Praise for *Responsible Dental Ownership*

If there is one thing that dental schools do very poorly it is preparing students for the business side of dentistry. Unfortunately, when one graduates they are often prone to getting advice, and possibly incentives, from the wrong sources and the ethics of the practice can suffer. This book should be on the curriculum of all dental schools in North America or, if not part of a course, listed as required reading! It will give the new graduate, and even those who have been in the practice for many years, the right perspective and tools to be both a good business owner and an upright and honest clinical dentist. The combination will certainly allow the dental owner to sleep better at night and feel fulfillment in his chosen profession.

—Brian D. Barrett, DDS, FACD, FICD, FPFA, FADI
Executive Director at Dental Association of PEI

I have been proud to open over nine dental practices and a dental lab in my 40-year career. I only wish I had Alex's book when I first started my journey. He offers the great perspective of the outsider looking in and observes dental practices with MBA eyes. He clarifies the importance of purpose as he leads readers through a clear, concise, and practical guide. Thank you for the courage and effort it took to produce this book!

—Dr Brian Friesen, DMD

T0145788

As a dental student, I find that we focus a lot of our time on the practical portion of dentistry: identifying symptoms, diagnosing, treating, and educating patients. We learn how to provide the best patient care. That being said, the business aspect is lightly touched upon throughout our education without any specific guidelines on how to actually manage a practice, let alone make it successful. This book does just that; it addresses and combines the business and patient care sides of dentistry, while providing tools and ideas to achieve a successful and responsible practice. I have yet to graduate and Zlatin's book has already revealed to me many behind-the-scenes actions that must take place and be established to lead a successful dental team and practice. I believe this should be a mandatory read to all dental students and practicing dentists, whether newly graduated or veterans. One could only benefit from this read.

—Dmitry Mikhlin
Dental Student at University of Manitoba

The many hats of business ownership are challenging for dentists to juggle when they spend their days delivering clinical care for patients. In this book, Zlatin delves into the challenge of being a dentist and a business owner, yet he manages to present his advice and information in a way that is very progressive and easy to understand. Zlatin ensures to align and draw parallels between a practice's patient care goals and the success of the business. This book is a great resource!

—Dr. Adam W. Pite BSc, DDS, FAGD, AFAAID

Alex Zlatin has made it his goal to consistently meet the needs of our dental practice. Alex has the unique understanding and overview of someone who not only works directly with dental practices, but someone who gets where we're coming from as business owners. Alex knows our successes and has been able to effectively articulate our struggles in his writing.

—Craig Hayes

Dental Office Manager at Deer Valley Dental Care

Dental Consultant at Dental Management Secrets

RESPONSIBLE DENTAL OWNERSHIP

ALEX ZLATIN

RESPONSIBLE
DENTAL
OWNERSHIP

Balancing Ethics and Business
THROUGH PURPOSE

Published by Advantage, Charleston, South Carolina.
Member of Advantage Media Group.

ADVANTAGE is a registered trademark, and the Advantage colophon is a trademark of Advantage Media Group, Inc.

Printed in the United States of America.

10 9 8 7 6 5 4 3 2 1

ISBN: 978-1-59932-860-7
LCCN: 2018934588

Book design by Megan Elger.

This publication is designed to provide accurate and authoritative information in regard to the subject matter covered. It is sold with the understanding that the publisher is not engaged in rendering legal, accounting, or other professional services. If legal advice or other expert assistance is required, the services of a competent professional person should be sought.

Advantage Media Group is proud to be a part of the Tree Neutral® program. Tree Neutral offsets the number of trees consumed in the production and printing of this book by taking proactive steps such as planting trees in direct proportion to the number of trees used to print books. To learn more about Tree Neutral, please visit **www.treeneutral.com**.

Advantage Media Group is a publisher of business, self-improvement, and professional development books and online learning. We help entrepreneurs, business leaders, and professionals share their Stories, Passion, and Knowledge to help others Learn & Grow. Do you have a manuscript or book idea that you would like us to consider for publishing? Please visit **advantagefamily.com** or call **1.866.775.1696**.

To Karina—for pushing me to be a better version of myself and for your support through our joint journey of life.

TABLE OF CONTENTS

PREFACE

Being responsible often implies having an obligation to do something or being the primary cause of something. This means you are morally accountable for your actions and can be blamed or credited for them. Owning a dental clinic puts you in an impossible situation when it comes to responsibility: you need to spend your days treating patients, but you also need to run the practice as a business.

Recent changes in the market and in regulation (and its enforcement), have exponentially increased the administrative overhead and increased risk and liability to a dental owner. The popularity of dental corporations, the emergence of young and savvy dental graduates, and recent economic changes (especially new tax policies and increased competition in big urban areas) have pushed dental owners outside the comfort zone of what's considered their responsibility.

Responsible Dental Ownership was written to uncover a different approach in running dental clinics. It shows how, instead of conflict, there can be a symbiosis between patient oral care and the operational excellence of the business. This starts with the simple concept of defining your purpose.

During my eleven years of management experience outside the dental industry, I made many mistakes but was fortunate to learn from all of them. After five years of working with dentists, it became clear to me that I could use my experience to help dentists and their staff on their journey to fulfillment and accomplishment. This book is a small part of my efforts to expose dentists and their staff members to the combination of elements that attract the right patients, build a solid team, and define and achieve goals.

I am thrilled you are reading my book and look forward to taking this journey with you.

—Alex Zlatin
November 2017

WHY RESPONSIBLE DENTAL OWNERSHIP?

In my five years as a company leader, I spoke to hundreds of dentists, office managers, and staff and identified a surprising fact: *they don't really know what to do when it comes to managing a dental practice.* Few dental practices have figured out the business side of the practice to a level where they are truly responsible for both the business side and the clinical side. The dentists, managers, and staff have different pieces, but no one has the full picture; if they do, they don't have the tools to implement the business organization needed. They can make enough money to survive, but they are not seeing their potential, achieving the best oral health for their patients, or maximizing their ability to make a profit.

In my experience, dentists fall into one of two groups. In the first are those who want to focus on dentistry and oral health and train themselves to be experts in the medical aspects of their jobs. They should find the right person to manage their practice for them, and deal with landlords, marketing, human resources (HR), financials, and the other elements of a practice. The second group consists of dentists who are more entrepreneurial. They are not trying to be world-renowned specialists but want a franchise of dental clinics. Their path necessitates acquiring the tools to be an entrepreneur, creating business processes, and building the right team. The majority of dentists fall somewhere in between these two groups, and their life looks muddied. If dentists do not know which type of dentist they are (group one or group two), they are stuck in the middle, doing a bit of what it takes to be both kinds of dentist but without consistency. This approach is rarely successful.

THE PROBLEM FACING THE DENTAL OWNER

Dental students spend years in school to become dentists in order to deal with oral health. They are not prepared to own a clinic and take on management-related tasks, such as marketing, branding, HR, hiring, firing, mentoring, and training. They are not trained to know how to run their practice efficiently, attract and retain patients, or manage wealth, income, and outflows. They do not know how to be landlords or property investors. In short, dentists don't have enough tools to succeed. Add to this the high stress of running a dental practice, and you, the dentist, know why you need help.

Furthermore, big dental corporations are starting to own more clinics and set goals and metrics, and young graduate associates are more profit oriented. This is pushing clinicians to mistreat the patients so that the business of dentistry is starting to have a negative connotation. In many ways, it has become "get it done or prescribe more to earn more profit and provide less customer service." Responsible dental ownership, however, means balancing medical treatment and business management. They are not mutually exclusive and you don't need to compromise, either. Just because you are running a business and have metrics and goals does not mean that you compromise on the patient's health.

Responsible Dental Ownership will help make you aware of the gaps in your business and provide you with some fundamental tools that are practical to implement. Many of you have probably attended clinical webinars or seminars, and some of you may have taken business courses for continuing education credits, but you still don't have practical tools to use when you come into your practice the next day. For example, you may learn that you need a morning meeting with staff, but many of you don't know how to explain why it's needed or how to lead the meeting. You don't know how to take advantage of what you learned.

Due to the amount of money that can be earned in this industry, many dentists become financially successful quickly but rarely acquire the business tools and experience needed to progress. This book will give you practical tools that you can use right away. For more extensive help, you can reach out to me for personalized support at alexzlatin.com.

WHY YOU NEED RESPONSIBLE DENTAL OWNERSHIP

This book is primarily written for dentists, owners of clinics, and office managers who are interested in how a dental practice should run. However, it will also help everyone in the dental industry who has a willingness to learn more about how a dental practice should be managed.

Many people are perplexed; they're not able to clearly define their problem, and they're clueless as to the right solution. I come from a business background with experience in many different types of environments, one of which included working in a company that services dentists. This experience afforded me the opportunity to analyze a lot of complaints and problems that dentists and dental staff members shared with me. I began to see the pitfalls, stressors and the structures that were unnecessarily causing the staff to be overwhelmed and I identified the skill sets needed to overcome them. This analysis helped me to form an understanding not just of the small problems of each office but also a problem common to all practices that falls into my area of expertise. This book discusses my analysis of the biggest problems facing dental owners and dental office managers, and provides practical solutions that can be implemented right away to reduce stressors and maximize the success of a dental practice. It offers practical tools and advice you can use without having to go to business school or gain years of managerial experience. Ultimately, as you acquire the knowledge and experience offered in the following pages, you'll not only turn your practice into a well-oiled, profitable business but you'll be able to reduce the stress of trying to be both a full-time dentist and a full-time business owner.

This book will appeal to several types of people: the dentist who owns a practice and is aware that something is not right or that something can be better, the dentist who does not yet own an office but would like to, and dental office managers and aspiring dental office managers. Other staff in the dental practice will also gain a better insight into what it feels like to be a dental owner and what dental owners' stressors are. In the chapters ahead, you will acquire knowledge and tools you can roll out to ensure you have an under-standing of marketing to attract and retain patients. Likewise, you'll learn how to write a job ad, how to mentor or train staff, set the right expectations, and hire and fire staff. By the end of the book, you'll have the knowledge and tools needed to practice responsible dental ownership.

CHAPTER 1

A DENTAL OWNER'S PURPOSE

A few years ago, I met Dr. Sanchez who was considered to be successful. By the time he reached middle age, he was running three full-time practices. When we met, we sat in his office discussing a variety of matters, but it was a comment toward the end of our conversation that piqued my interest. "As an owner," he said, "I don't even know what report I should be reading."

Having a business background and working in a dental software company for over five years allowed me to have many business conversations with dentists and office managers. In those conversations, statements like that are made from time to time. However, hearing this from a successful dentist with three practices really struck a chord with me. It gave me a solid grasp of the fact that regardless of how many practices dentists might have, regardless of how successful they might be considered, they still lack an understanding of business functions in which they were never trained.

The pieces fell into place for me. I understood that as the dental schools and associations were not willing to address these issues, some other source of knowledge and understanding of owning and running a business was needed. I needed to share information with dental industry professionals to help them feel more in control. The feeling that you are in control is important, and to have this feeling you need to know your purpose.

But what is your purpose? Dentists spend about eight hours treating patients in the operatory, sometimes more. They don't live the day-to-day administration side of the practice. They don't gain that experience. They don't fail quickly enough in the beginning to learn from their mistakes. They rarely gain experience in managing employees or seeing how their customer service affects patients. At the end of a long work week, they would have to stay after hours to find out if their business is doing well. Even if they were to stay, they wouldn't know what to look for. This is because they do not have much, if any, education or experience in reviewing the financials of a business in general and a dental practice in particular.

In management, early experience involves many mistakes and learning opportunities. It takes a certain maturity and self-awareness to leverage these mistakes into an experience from which you can learn. This experience helps you make fewer mistakes and better decisions. For dentists, this is the equivalent to getting out of school. They know, in general, how to diagnose and how to treat, but it is only with experience (and some mistakes in diagnosis and/or treatment) that they learn to be better dentists. The same happens with management skills. As they do not have the opportunity to gain experience by making mistakes, they are prone to continue to make poor management decisions.

In addition to not knowing what to look for, dental practices are, generally, financially forgiving, which means dentists often don't realize they need to look closely at their financials. Usually, a lot of money is coming in, so as dentists pull their own salary, they believe themselves to be successful, but they don't know how successful they could be with a little bit of management know-how.

Dr. Sanchez told me he didn't know what to look for, how to learn which reports to review, or how to read them. I could have told him what to look for, what information to glean, how to interpret it, and how to fix problems, but this wasn't the solution. It would

Definition of a Dental Practice: A corporation owned by a dentist who usually also practices dentistry. He may employ one or more associates, who do not share in the ownership of the practice. There are many possible internal structures to dental practices. Other structures include a dental corporation owned by multiple dentists.

only have added to his workload an area of management inconsistent with his specialty and passion without necessarily increasing his sense of control. Dentists who are owners know they should look at the numbers and be responsible for the business, but this isn't what makes them happy. They're happy doing dentistry, not analyzing metrics. So what can they do about that?

BEFORE YOU KNOW WHO YOU ARE, YOU HAVE TO KNOW WHO YOU ARE NOT

When I was still in high school, I became close friends with a family in my neighborhood. Two of the sons owned a heating and cooling company and they did the installations themselves. Every once in a while, they would ask me to help them lift equipment onto the roofs, hand them tools, and do generally helpful tasks. They paid me something, which was fine. I helped them. They were friends. It was nice.

One year, they asked me to help them throughout the summer because it was their busiest season. I didn't have much to do then, and I wanted to earn some cash, so I worked with them. It was my first real-world job, and I was extremely excited.

It was quickly clear to all of us that I didn't share their aptitude for craftsmanship. They tried to teach me so that they could rely on me more, but it was clear that it was not for me. I wasn't passionate about it. I wasn't excited to do more, and their teaching didn't sink in. It just wasn't working.

One day, they got a call from a Russian-speaking client. Not knowing the language was a deal breaker for this client. I did speak Russian so they handed me the phone and asked me to explain their system, which I was easily able to do. That was a eureka moment. It became clear to the three of us that the biggest contribution I could make to their business was by doing something that had nothing to do with installations or craftsmanship. The next day, I sold two systems to new clients, something the company owners found challenging because their skills weren't in sales or administration. That was where they were lacking.

I transitioned to the office where I made sales calls and took customer support calls in different languages. I was extremely happy with that. It was rewarding to do something well and see the fruits of my efforts. The owners were happy because they were able to focus on their specialty, knowing they had someone to do what they couldn't do. That particular summer, I helped them triple their business, which meant they could hire two full-time assistants to help install the systems I had sold.

The reason that we were able to achieve that level of success was by creating synergy between the people who did the technical work and the person handling the office, sales closure, customer service, and the paperwork. I enjoyed it. It came naturally to me despite my young age and relative inexperience. It allowed them to deliver top-notch work based on their specialty. It was a win-win for everyone. There was trust and understanding. Everyone focused on what they did best.

The moral of the story is that success can be achieved if the staff focuses on what they are good at. I was good at administration and sales, so I was able to realize my potential there and make a better contribution. Similarly, a dentist dealing with administration is not going to reach his potential as a dentist unless he gets the right people to run the practice. The story of my friends' company is an example of the synergy that must exist in a dental practice. People should be put in roles they're passionate about. These are the roles that naturally fit their skill set and come with responsibilities on which they are happy to focus.

The solution for Dr. Sanchez was to show him how he could benefit from having a trusted office manager who could do the administrative work for him. In this way, he could focus on what he did best, and the office manager could review numbers with him on a monthly basis.

The key for the dental owner is finding an office manager who can be trusted. Without trust, you have nothing, and building trust requires an ongoing effort on both sides. Once established, the office manager can understand what information the owner needs to feel comfortable that the business is doing well.

A DENTIST OF MANY HATS

Dentists have three hats, which they wear on different occasions. The first one is the most straightforward: *the clinician hat,* the hat of the dentist as a treatment provider, the hat in which the dentist spends most of his time, the hat he wears as the income producer for his own business. For the majority of dentists, this is their favorite hat because they are extremely passionate about being a clinician.

I once asked a friend of mine why he chose to go to dental school. "Dentists make a very nice living," he answered, "so money is why I went." He's now in his third year of dental school and his tune has changed slightly. "The money could be great," he said more recently, "but there's so much I'm learning. I like doing this. I like forming crowns. I like everything about the practice." He, like most of his fellow students, were undergoing this kind of transformation and growing more passionate about the clinical aspect of dentistry.

His story shows that even if a student is lured into dental school by the prospect of high earnings, passion is key. As students go through dental school, the passion to be an actual dentist keeps growing. Unfortunately, so does their debt. When they graduate, they work as an associate in an established practice under the supervision of a veteran dentist, which allows them to repay their college debt and gain treatment experience. Often, while working as an associate, they'll revive the dream they once had to own a dental practice, but seeing how older dentists run their practice may lead them to question if there is a better way. They may think more money could be made if the business were run better. By the time their college debt is paid off, an opportunity may arise for them to open their own clinic or buy into one. This is when everything changes.

Many aspiring dentists have the feeling that they know exactly what needs to be done and how to do it, but they don't know what ownership entails. They don't know how to evaluate whether they're running a successful practice, what is considered a successful practice, and where to start. That is just the tip of the iceberg. This is when the dentist has to don a second hat.

The business owner hat demands business acumen and a certain level of financial understanding. Dentists need to understand investment because they have invested money in buying, or buying into, a practice. Most dentists who buy a practice do not have these skills.

The administrative hat, the third hat, is the most confusing. It involves office management and operations management. It includes customer service, HR, privacy regulations, marketing and branding, and interior design. It also includes running the day-to-day business, processing incoming patients, managing accounts receivable, handling banking and cash, and troubleshooting third-party vendors, such as insurance companies.

If dentists spend eight hours a day in the clinician's hat and two hours a day in the owner's hat, how many hours do they have to spend in the administrative hat? Probably not many, and this is why practices fall apart. In the worst cases, they go out of business. In the best-case scenario, they hire someone who is stellar at operations and their dental corporation grows from one practice to three practices to five practices, all managed by an office manager who grew into the role of operations director.

The majority of scenarios generally fall in between. Often, newly hired office managers don't know exactly what needs to be done, and this leads to a lack of trust between them and the dentist. At other times, office managers aren't given enough free rein. For example, they need to run the day-to-day affairs but cannot approve a $30 purchase or use the company credit card. Not only does a tight leash indicate and foster a lack of trust, it also limits the ability of the person who's responsible for the operations to run it efficiently. This is a lose-lose scenario.

The fundamental problem is that dentists graduate and get to the point of owning a business without first acquiring any of the practical tools necessary to own a business. Then, if they are smart enough to decide to hire someone to take care of the business, they discover it's very hard to find someone qualified to manage the unique qualities of a dental office. Unfortunately, there are no schools to train people specifically in dental office management. Similarly for dentists, there are no classes in the dental college curriculum to teach them how to manage a dental office or understand financial management at even its most basic level, such as how to interpret a profit and loss (P&L) report or how to make one in the first place.

THE THREE DRIVERS OF THE DENTAL PRACTICE

Since a dental practice is one where the owner is also the income producer, dental owners spend most of their day being an employee. They carry the weight of the business loans, and are left holding the bag when an office manager resigns or is fired. This makes the office manager central to the success of the practice. It's not possible to take an office manager from a non-dental business, drop that person into a dental practice, and expect him or her to swim. Why is this?

A dental office manager needs to understand what I call the three drivers of a dental practice—that is, the systems of the practice that make it different from other practices and businesses. They comprise 1) scheduling hygiene appointments, 2) identifying problems that require treatment and managing the treatment schedule, and 3) managing accounts receivable.

The first driver relates to the structure of a dental practice and the appointments that need to be properly tracked. For example, hygiene appointments, the cleaning appointments that every patient needs, should be booked in advance for each patient in order to ensure repeat business and that the patient's oral health is properly maintained. Advance scheduling of clients' bi-annual cleaning visits makes it easier to bring them back, and this regularity allows them to develop a relationship with the hygienist.

The second driver involves the dentist doing an exam at the end of the cleaning, which can identify a need for future treatment, such as crowns, extractions, and bridges. This means you can book appointments for patients for particular treatments. This is where the office generates the big money and any discovered oral health issues can be resolved before they worsen.

All of these appointments need to be tracked on the administrative side to make sure that insurance pre-authorization and approval is in place, which brings us to the third driver: tracking insurance payments. Insurance covers the majority of all the treatments that are done by the office.

These three drivers must have adequate resources allocated to them to maximize income. The drivers must be monitored and managed by an office manager who understands the unique nature of a dental practice. In Chapter 2, we'll look in more detail at the structure and responsibilities of a dental office manager, and in

Chapter 3, we'll look in more detail at the drivers of a practice, how a dental practice is structured, and how it differs from other businesses.

FINDING YOUR PURPOSE

Simon Sinek, a British American bestselling author, motivational speaker, and marketing consultant, wrote *Start with Why*, which describes why company leaders need to establish their purpose—that is, *why* a company does what it does, and why individuals do what they do. People generally start the other way around: they begin with the *what* and then the *how* of the business before they finally get to the *why*, if at all.

In a dental practice, the dentist is the owner, the face, and the name on the practice's door, but he or she is looking into patients' mouths full-time, which means having to hire an office manager or operations manager to run the business on a daily basis. Because of the unique setup of a dental practice, the dental owner needs to determine the *why*—that is, the purpose of the practice and his or her vision and, out of that, develop the *how* and the *what* of the practice.

When I accepted the leadership role at Maxim Software Systems, I realized that the company didn't have a purpose or vision, which allowed me the flexibility to create one. Creating a purpose and a vision for the company made me first think about my personal purpose, my own *why*, and that allowed me connect with myself on a deeper level than I'd experienced before.

When I was in the process of discovering my *why*, I spoke with my closest friends and family members to get their feedback: why did they believe that I do what I do? It wasn't easy to talk to my closest people and ask them this question. Nevertheless, it was an interesting and rewarding journey. I learned that I thrive when I help other people succeed. I feel fulfilled when I see how my advice contributes to another's success. I deduced that my purpose is to help other people to succeed by offering advice. My business purpose therefore became empowering clients through intelligent software and exceptional service offered by Maxim Software Systems.

Leveraging that knowledge and using Maxim to empower clients was a natural progression for me. Natural doesn't mean easy. In fact, it was one of the most difficult tasks I've ever done.

When running a company, it's important to achieve clarity of purpose between the business owner and the rest of the people in the organization. This gives everyone a clear guideline throughout their day and helps them in their decision-making processes. The dental owner or office manager cannot be with all of the employees all day long to ensure that they're making the right decisions. When employees are not sure what decision to make, having them understand and follow established guidelines allows them to choose the option that empowers the patient. Clarity of purpose helps the business

My Purpose: My *why* and the company's *why* had to be aligned. My purpose is to help other people to succeed by offering advice; my company's purpose was to empower clients through intelligent software and exceptional service. A similar alignment should occur between the dental clinic staff and the owner.

owner find the right office manager to help run the business. This clarity of purpose should be communicated to all staff to create alignment throughout the practice.

It's very difficult to just say, "You do this, then you do that, and now you have purpose." Finding purpose is a process that each individual needs to undergo. Sometimes, people can do it with minimal guidance; others need help. It's not unusual for dental owners to not know how to find their purpose; they often work with the office manager or their spouse to define it together.

If you are stuck, Simon Sinek's website has a small but powerful exercise that helps individuals define their purpose.[1]

EXPRESSING YOUR PURPOSE

Communicating your purpose, your *why*, to your office manager, whether that person is already in your practice or is newly hired, is important. Because office managers are the people who run the practice while the dental owner tends to patients, they must serve the practice's purpose and do so on behalf of the dental owner.

Office managers who buy into, and believe in, the practice's purpose can instruct all staff in that purpose so they know what needs to be done, create the necessary processes, and guide their colleagues to achieve goals.

We'll look at the dentist-office manager relationship in more detail in Chapter 2.

---

1   For more information, visit https://www.startwithwhy.com/LearnYour-Why.aspx.

THREE EXERCISES ABOUT PURPOSE-

This chapter addresses the importance of having a purpose. It explores how finding your *why* is a journey, not something explained in a few lines, or even a whole book.

A personal journey begins with the understanding that you are going to undergo a very private and deep process with yourself. You might not like what you find, but in the end, you will know yourself in a very intimate way. After going through this process myself, I can definitely say the journey is worth it.

There are three exercises that you should do to bring yourself closer to finding your purpose.

1. THE MIRROR EXERCISE

Reflect back to the times you have felt the most

    a.   joy

    b.   thrill

    c.   self-confidence

You should do this exercise multiple times. We best remember situations that are connected to emotion, good and bad, but you should focus on the good. Uncovering bad memories is valuable for understanding what you are not.

Use the commonalities among the memories to help you with your first step to your *why*.

2. THE FRIENDS EXERCISE

Pick up to three of your closest friends and ask them why are they friends with you.

Initially, their reasons will sound generic, so make it difficult for them and challenge them to make their reasons clearer and more personal.

Toward the end of the exercise, you will usually find they explain how being friends with you makes them feel.

This is another step in your journey of understanding more about yourself and your purpose.

3. THE TRIAL AND ERROR EXERCISE

Now that you have learned about what prompts strong positive feelings and what strong and positive feelings you create in others, it is time to put this to a test.

This exercise requires that you find the correlation between the two previous exercises. For example, when doing the first exercise, I realized I had strong feelings whenever I was able to help people achieve their goals, whether that was helping my buddies grow their business or training new crew members in the navy to help them pass their examinations. Looking at other people's results gave me feelings of pride, fulfillment, and self-confidence.

In the second exercise, my friends explained that they loved my ability to quickly dissect a situation and present it in a non-emotional way. That helped them see the solution clearly and quickly. They felt comfortable coming to me with their problems (business and personal). They felt that I could be trusted with their dilemmas, could help them see a solution, and could guide them as the situation evolved.

In the third exercise, I connected the other two exercises to show me my purpose and my passion. In my case, I consciously tried to help people who were not close friends see how their success made me feel. Once you are able to replicate these feelings in future actions, it's like a drug: you just want more. If I could experience this level of positive and strong emotions with people I hardly knew, I had found my purpose.

Now it's your turn. You'll know if you've found your purpose by how you feel after you take action.

CHAPTER 2

EMPOWERING YOUR OFFICE MANAGER

During a business trip to Alberta, I visited the dental practice of a client, Dr. Charlton. He knew I was coming, but when I arrived, I met the office manager instead. The dentist was working on an emergency patient. I hadn't met the office manager before, as she'd only recently taken on the role. I was curious to get to know her. She came from an administrative background in a global logistics corporation but, later, decided to study to be a dental assistant. After graduation, she came to Dr. Charlton's practice, where she had been working for about two years. She wasn't passionate about being a dental assistant and, partially due to her business background, saw herself in the role of running and managing the dental practice. When Dr. Charlton offered her an opportunity to manage his practice, she jumped on it. When I asked how it was going, she said, "Well, I'm not sure as to what I need to be doing exactly. Everything's a bit of a mess, but we're dealing with it one day at a time." I wasn't really surprised, because I'd seen this situation before.

This story illustrates many problems that dental practices face: failure to communicate the *why* or purpose and failing to clearly define roles and responsibilities.

In this case, the dental owner hadn't communicated the *why* to her because he didn't have a *why*. The practice was failing on this point.

Her role was also ill defined. There had been no discussion about her accountability or responsibility. There were no clear expectations, which left her in a state of confusion because she wasn't sure what needed to be done. She was dealing with it one day at a time, but this meant she was just being reactive. When I asked the dentist and the office manager the simple question, "What is it that needs to be done?" neither knew how to answer. This is how a lot of dental offices are: they're just reacting to what comes up.

Now, it's easy to name a few routine tasks that are done by the front staff, but the person in charge of running and leading the practice must have bigger goals, see what needs to be done on a larger scale, and know how to achieve this vision. A *why* is not something that is achievable. It is a guide that helps us on a daily basis. It is the motivation and the reason we achieve the *what*. This must be very clear, and there must be clarity to ensure what needs to be done is completed.

Not being able to clearly communicate what is expected of the office manager makes it impossible to determine the skill set needed. Most dentists can't evaluate an office manager or that person's qualifications for the job. This is a common problem in the dental industry.

While it's clear one of the first roles that needs to be filled in every dental practice is that of the office manager, I've found that less than 50 percent of dental practices have one. This in itself shows that the dental owner does not see any value in having such a position or paying a salary for the role. The ones who do have an office manager often become dissatisfied with him or her, partly because they've been unable to explain their vision and unable to clearly communicate their expectations, which means they were unable to develop a positive relationship and trust between themselves and their managers.

Therefore, understanding why you need an office manager and knowing how to communicate responsibilities and the vision of the practice is central to the dental owner's success.

WHY YOU NEED AN *EMPOWERED* OFFICE MANAGER

The first very obvious reason why a dental owner should have an office manager, or an individual who's responsible for running the practice properly, is that the dental owner cannot be at two places at the same time. Dentists spend their day in the back, so they're not aware of what is going on in the front, what's being done, what's not being done, or how their patients are being treated. This makes finding a capable individual who believes in the dental office's purpose crucial. A shared vision strengthens the connection between the dental owner and the manager and will make the manager more passionate about pursuing the purpose, or vision, of the dental practice.

When the dentist's vision, or purpose, is clearly defined, communicated, and imbued in the office manager, both dentist and manager end up doing whatever it takes to ensure there is progress toward that vision.

Practices without Purpose

Sadly, it is difficult to find a dental practice with a real purpose that is communicated to the staff. If you search on Google for "dental clinic vision mission," you'll find plenty. However, they all make the same promises: we provide great service, treat you like family, use the most advanced technology, and will always be honest. The following are a few real examples:

Our team of experts provides a wide range of excellent services, from routine preventative dentistry to complex restorative work. We use the most advanced materials and techniques. We care about our patients and always stand behind our work.

We are friendly dentists who want to provide you with quality dental care in a caring and professional environment.

Our aim is to make you feel at home and comfortable in our beautiful office.

Our team takes pride in our expert dental services. We are happy to serve our many long-time patients and look forward to welcoming new patients to our office.

These listings are all examples of the *what* (dental services) and the *how* (friendly services, beautiful office, feel at home, professional environment). They list reasons to visit them, but none list their *why*. This means they are no different than the other clinics that offer the same services. Few clinics demonstrate a real purpose.

To inspire patients or potential patients, the dental owner must first empower employees to do whatever it takes. This means a level of trust must be developed over time. This is a good reason to hire an office manager early on. Second, the office manager must be capable of taking the purpose, the *why* of the practice, to develop the *how*. That is, the office manager must figure out how to ensure that processes are implemented in order to progress toward the dental office's vision.

> **The office manager must be capable of taking the purpose, the *why* of the practice, to develop the *how*. That is, the office manager must figure out how to ensure that processes are implemented in order to progress toward the dental office's vision.**

An office manager also allows the dental owner to plan for the long term. At the end of the day, a dental owner may want to focus on expanding the practice, probably to more locations. Alternatively, the dental owner may want to focus on dentistry, the medical aspects of dentistry, or on specializing in a particular segment of dentistry. As the practice grows, the dental owner must already have developed that trust and relationship with the office manager, who runs the business side of the practice on a day-to-day basis. The better the mutual understanding of what is being done and what needs to be done, the stronger their trust of each other and their relationship will be, and the better able they will be to prepare for the long term.

HOW TO FIND A CAPABLE OFFICE MANAGER

Most dentists find it difficult to find a capable, knowledgeable, experienced individual for the position of dental office manager. No formal education to teach the necessary skills exists. The reality in Canada is that little distinction is made between general office administrators and dental office managers, who require specific skills and knowledge. Because they're acting as general managers, they need a unique understanding of business operations management, marketing, and financials, but this is not being taught to office administrators. As was the case with Dr. Charlton's office manager, individuals coming from a high-end administrative role in a logistics corporation will find few of their skills relevant to what is required to successfully run a dental practice.

The majority of office managers are receptionists who have been working in some capacity in the dental practice for many years. Other staff members from within the practice, such as a dental assistant, are also often promoted to the position of office manager, which was the case at Dr. Charlton's practice. Many employees assume it involves less work because they don't know what the position entails. They often think that an office manager just tells people what to do. They assume it's a promotion because it's better money and thus assume that they're going up the ladder.

Some dentists bring their spouses to this role, regardless of their background, because they feel they can trust them more. Neither, however, knows what the role requires. In a very high-stress environment, bringing your marriage to work isn't always the best idea, and this has lead to many divorces.

In each of these scenarios, not having clarity, not understanding what office management entails, and not having the skills required for the job is a problem with which most practices struggle. I have seen this so many times I decided to figure out how to best help practices find qualified office managers.

I arrived at the idea of having a professional association for Canadian dental office managers, which I launched in 2015. Today, the Canadian Association of Dental Office Managers helps its Canadian members with educational webinars and a member-only forum that serves as a sounding board to increase awareness of what being a dental office manager really means. The purpose for this association is to bring some respect to that position, to bring some clarity to what it entails, and to create a community of individuals who are passionate about office management in a dental environment. The association aims to create standards for the knowledge required. With our certification, the dentist can at least know that the office manager has some level of understanding of what it takes to run a practice. This will make finding capable individuals to man that position easier.

If you are experiencing challenges in hiring the right staff, go to www.officemanagers.ca to see if you qualify for a free membership in this association.

SIX KEY ELEMENTS IN EVERY DENTAL PRACTICE

There are six key elements in every dental practice: the three drivers we introduced in Chapter 1 and will explore in more detail in Chapter 3, and an additional three elements. The first element is directly connected to the first driver, the second element to the second driver, and the third element to the third driver. The remaining elements have to do with customer service, HR, marketing, and general business operations. These six points are the foundation of what a dental office manager needs to know and achieve.

1. Hygiene (cleaning) appointments, which we established as the first driver of a dental practice, are a must, and have to be managed well to have a successful dental practice. Each active patient needs to have regular cleaning appointments (and dental exam). To achieve this goal, a tracking system should be established that schedules the next appointment (usually every six months) after completing the current hygiene appointment, accompanied by an appointment reminder system. Such systems ensure a full schedule for all hygienists. If the hygiene schedule is not almost at capacity, income is being lost, the practice is not growing as it could be, and thus is not as successful as it could be. It is imperative that all patients have scheduled hygiene appointments because proper and consistent hygiene appointments are essential to maintaining adequate oral health.

2. Tracking future treatments, which we established as the second driver of a dental practice, requires an understanding of how treatments are classified (basic, major) and of insurance company coverage and payment processes. (There has been a change in the insurance approval procedure. Now, instead of the approval documents being sent to the clinic, they are sent to patients). Although there are rarely problems getting approval for basic treatments—and they often can be booked right away—major treatments require pre-authorization and are followed up with the patients to make sure they have received the insurance approval in the

mail. Once patients have the insurance approval, they are able to book an appointment for treatment.

3. Accounts receivable, which is the third driver of a dental practice, must be kept to a minimum. Insurance covers roughly 70 percent of treatments. Therefore, it is necessary to track which insurance company owes you what and for which patients. Understanding when to expect those amounts is key to cash flow stability. One form of action may involve collecting the amount owed from the patients, after treatment, and letting them deal with claiming reimbursement from the insurance company.

In addition to these three drivers are the following three key elements that make up the six, in total, that support a successful dental practice:

1. A safe and inviting environment must be maintained for patients and staff. This includes the design of the office, branding, customer service, and HR.

2. The dental owner and all staff members must do everything to promote proper oral health for all patients. The nature of the business is dentistry, oral health. This must be in the minds of every staff member at all times. New patient acquisition must be balanced with patient attrition, mortality, and an aging patient base. The type of dentistry you do, the types of procedure, and therefore your income, are dependent on the oral health of your patients, which may be related to their age. Older patients need more implants, dentures or partial dentures than younger patients. However, it is important to know what your patient base looks like in terms of age and then make

sure you're attracting enough patients of all age groups. A lot of dental offices overlook this important point because they're caught up in the day-to-day reactive approach to running the office, but you need to look at the long term. If you do not have enough new patients to compensate for patient losses and an aging patient base, you end up with a dying practice. Eventually, the practice will not have enough patients. The office manager needs to make sure that these issues are looked at and action is taken.

3. It is important to be able to handle the finances of the practice. This means being able to read and interpret different financial reports—whether it's a P&L or a cash flow report—and being able to determine which ratios are applicable to the business. You need to look at them every once in a while, understand what they mean, and be able to develop an action plan on that basis.

When we had the first advisory board meeting for the Dental Office Managers Association of Canada, about six office managers came to a consensus that the number-one skill that all people who consider themselves office managers lack is the ability to read and interpret financial reports. Some didn't know it was their job to read them; others didn't understand how to interpret and analyze reports in order to take action. An empowered office manager handles not just a few or most, but all six key elements.

THE DOCTOR-OFFICE MANAGER RELATIONSHIP

About a month or so after my visit to Dr. Sanchez, his office manager asked me to help with some issues she'd been experiencing. At the meeting, the first question she asked was what the dentist and I had talked about when we had previously met. This was interesting because it showed that there was no trust between the dentist and the office manager.

This is unfortunate, but it showcases how distrust and lack of communication can cause confusion and stress for staff members.

THE NUMBER-ONE RELATIONSHIP INGREDIENT: TRUST

What is trust? What does it mean in business? What does it mean in a dental office business? Trust is knowing that a particular individual will behave in a certain way when faced with a particular situation. It means having confidence in someone to make decisions you would approve of. It means knowing someone extremely well.

> Trust is knowing that a particular individual will behave in a certain way when faced with a particular situation.

In general, achieving this level of trust with a life partner is considered the crowning achievement of a marriage and of life, so it's no surprise that this is the goal of managers, executives, and business owners worldwide.

When I joined Maxim Software Systems as CEO, I met with the owner to discuss the importance of setting mutual expectations in order to understand the risks to which one of us might subject the other. It was important to discuss our mutual goals, and from that, develop a working arrangement with which we both felt comfortable. I expected to be the company leader, the ultimate decision maker. In this capacity, the owner needed to trust me enough to give me the authority I needed. I had to promise him, in return, to bring to his attention dilemmas and the critical decisions I had to make *before* making them.

A lot of people given power and authority wrongly believe they cannot show weakness or vulnerability. They think that the person giving them the authority and power must always see them make the right decisions. The reality is that we're human, and we make mistakes. We make decisions based on the information we have to hand.

> A lot of people given power and authority wrongly believe they cannot show weakness or vulnerability.

It's important to know that showing vulnerability and being aware that you are human and that you make mistakes doesn't make you weaker or a less of a leader. It shows that you are aware of your weaknesses, and you are trying to mitigate risks. Being open, honest, genuine, and not afraid of showing vulnerability was one of the best decisions I have made in my life because it allowed me to see that I didn't have less authority by collaborating. Working with another person doesn't mean I have less power. On the contrary, it gives me an opportunity to validate my thought process and validate my decision-making processes with an individual who shares the vision and the purpose.

Everyone is different. We all have our own thought processes and our own set of experiences and knowledge, yet we can share a common vision and purpose. If my business partner felt something was wrong, he would stop me and express his opinion, which is wonderful.

It is important that office managers and dental owners understand that this is important because it allows them to see how their own brain works and allows them to recognize how their experiences and knowledge guide them in the decisions they make.

This has worked well in our company. We've never had a situation where we couldn't see the other's viewpoint. We put a lot of time and effort into reiterating and explaining our viewpoint because we believe this is the key to a good, solid relationship.

The reality is that trust is not an outcome; it's a daily effort made by both parties to enhance and maintain a relationship.

> **The reality is that trust is not an outcome; it's a daily effort made by both parties to enhance and maintain a relationship.**

FIVE STEPS TO CREATING A STRONG RELATIONSHIP

The formula I use to establish good relationships and maintain them is very simple.

Step 1 is defining your purpose, which we covered in Chapter 1. It's important to start here because without purpose, it's difficult to maintain relationships.

Step 2 is understanding others' purpose, their *why*. If they don't have one, try to help them define it. Communicating this purpose is very important, just as it's important that you share a purpose. If you don't, it's going to be difficult to develop a relationship.

Step 3 is defining and communicating what it is that you expect from the other party. What are the desired outcomes? What do you see being achieved by the other person's work?

Step 4 is understanding what others expect from you. What do they want to see as an outcome based on your work?

Step 5 is meeting frequently to share progress or challenges. If the best way to schedule a meeting is a calendar invite, then do that. If what works in your environment is multiple, five-minute conversations throughout the day, do that. The only rule to this step is to keep communicating and meeting. The majority of relationship failures are either because people feel that if there is no progress, there's either no point in meeting, or they just don't have time to meet, which means they have other things they consider to be higher priorities. However, if you don't prioritize meetings, if you don't have good relationships with other staff, and you don't have their trust, none of those other things you think are priorities will matter.

RELATIONSHIP CHALLENGES

As part of my executive director role in the Dental Office Manager Association, I've surveyed dental office managers and observed their main challenges. One of the mandatory requirements in the registration process is that prospective members list their top three challenges. From there, it is easy to deduce the common ones.

The number-one challenge that comes up is *not feeling appreciated by the owner.* If the owner is not aware of what it is that you do, there's little to appreciate. This is also related to trust: no trust means no relationship and no relationship means no appreciation. Dental owners should make an effort to establish a deep, meaningful relationship with their office managers to make them comfortable communicating their progress and challenges so that the dental practice isn't shadowed or clouded by lack of trust.

The second top challenge is staff turnover, which has been attributed to lack of mutual purpose or goal, lack of trust, unclear communication resulting in misunderstandings and increased stress. Again, the survey findings show the importance of being able to establish a positive relationship and high level of trust in the dental practice.

DETERMINING RESPONSIBILITY

Being aware of the work that needs to be done and the fact that someone needs to be responsible for it is not as easy as it sounds.

While participating in a small seminar for dental office managers, I asked the participants if they were aware that they were responsible for marketing. It seemed to be a simple question, but the majority of them were not aware that marketing was their responsibility. The ones who did know assumed that "being responsible" meant having a third-party company handle it.

Being responsible means that good work is done in line with purpose. These elements are equally important.

At the end of the day, someone needs to be responsible for marketing. The same goes for HR, privacy, financials, and all other business-related aspects of the practice.

Who do you think should be responsible for it? The dentist, who is supposed to be booked solid and generating revenue, or the person whose job is to run and manage the practice?

The reality is that the majority of dentists, as intelligent as they are and as resourceful as they can be, are not able to properly train the office manager in all areas of dental practice management. A lot of dentist don't know how to do this work, never mind train people to do it. This means the practice is run by a dental owner and an office manager, both of whom are ill equipped to be responsible and accountable for all the components involved in running a dental clinic.

Trust comes into play here again. The office manager is hired to take care of all aspects of the business, while the dentist focuses on clinical treatment. Because there is no proper education for dental office managers and because most office managers in dental clinics have been promoted from within—the receptionist, hygienist or dental assistant—they lack the understanding of how this new role is different from their previous one.

Meanwhile, dental owners' perception is that if they hire someone to do a particular job, then that person knows how to do it. It's a mistake to make this assumption. My motto is trust no one and question or double-check everything until people have earned your trust.

The quickest way to lose trust in people at work is to put them in positions they are not properly equipped to perform. In many cases, unfortunately, neither the dentist nor office manager is aware of this situation.

Seeing a person you've known for over fifteen years fail in a new role is tough. This happened with Dr. Beckham. His office manager was his wife and the mother of his children.

He originally reached out to me, inquiring about new software for his practice. He thought that his existing solution had stopped being relevant and did not provide any of the new features that are standard today, such as digital charting, patient communication, and point-of-sale integration.

An hour into our conversation, I discovered that software was the least of his concerns. He took over a practice and entrusted his wife to run it, but it had been stagnating since the day he took it over.

For those of you who are married, you probably empathize with Dr. Beckham's complex situation. There are, in my experience, only two outcomes here.

1. Separation and hiring a new office manager. This does not necessarily solve the problem as the new office manager might not be any better. This amplifies the stress of a separation or divorce for the dentist and the additional financial strain in case there's child support to be paid.

2. Hire an assistant to the office manager. If the office manager has too much to do, an assistant is the perfect solution. However, this is a pacifist solution that may require some dishonesty between the spouses. It is not a bad solution, but it may lead to a power struggle between the spouse and assistant.

Dr. Beckham chose the second path. His wife was able to take a step back from running the practice as the assistant took more and more responsibilities and was able to work with Dr. Beckham to help the practice grow and evolve. This is by far one of the best endings to this situation.

Quite a few of these situations result in divorce, so it is very important to ensure that your office manager/spouse has the tools, drive, and experience to take it on. Giving your spouse this book would be a great place to start.

DISCUSSING EXPECTATIONS

Dental owners need to realistically share what they expect of the office manager and, in turn, the office manager needs to share what they expect of the staff. Similar communication needs to occur between the office manager and the staff. One example of this is telling hygienists to book at least 75 percent of their patients for their next cleaning. This touches upon the first of the seven key points of properly running a practice: handling hygiene appointments properly. Setting this as a goal is reasonable and measurable. It's important to set this expectation early on, so your expectations are clear.

Once the dental owner and office manager agree on the purpose, the *why*, of the practice, and agree on expectations and desired outcomes, the dental owner must give the office manager the authority to function properly and implement practices that fulfill the dental owner's vision.

To make sure the dentist actually sees the expected results or is at least aware of the challenges, the office manager must take step 5 of the Five Steps to Creating a Strong Relationship (Chapter 2): frequently meeting and talking about everything.

Every time you make a point of checking that you and your staff are on the same page, you learn about the challenges facing the practice. You know what has been accomplished, what has not. You know what is going to be done. This needs to be very clear. The office manager is there to execute. The dental owner is there to do clinical work and observe how and what is being executed in the office. If everyone is competent and clear on responsibility and trust is being developed, this scenario should work out perfectly.

WHAT MATTERS MOST

Throughout my professional career, if I was given a nickel for every occasion when people tell me I cannot do everything myself and suggest I try delegating, I'd be swimming in an ocean of coins. The truth is that wearing too many hats is tiring, frustrating, and leads to burnout. Adrenaline can only carry you so far.

In many of my previous roles, I had trust issues and needed to make sure everything was done properly. I felt any failure was my failure, and I was determined to do whatever it took to prevent this. However, as I evolved as a manager and leader, I understood that by trying to do everything, I was bound to fail because there was just too much for one person to do. I started following the steps to build trust and set proper expectations. It has been a bumpy road, but it has resulted in many more wins.

As a dentist, your main focus should be on the clinical aspects of your practice, providing the best diagnostics and treatments for your patients. This means you must make someone you trust be responsible and accountable for all other aspects of the business. Having such an individual creates peace of mind, strengthens your sense of control, reduces stress, and gives you a sense of accomplishment and pride in your clinic. The following chapter will cover the main components that drive success in dental practices so that you may incorporate them into your own business.

CHAPTER 3

THE THREE DRIVERS OF A RESPONSIBLE PRACTICE

I have the saddest experiences—which can sometimes be humorous—when I take a dentist and/or an office manager to a successful clinic. The purpose of these visits is benchmarking. Seeing is believing, so it's important for us to see success in practice.

Often, when the dental owner or office manager sees how well the other practice is run and how in control the staff members are in terms of hygiene, diagnosis, future treatments, and accounts receivable, they create excuses for why they cannot reach this level of functionality. However, the three drivers are fundamental to the success of a dental practice, as we will explore in this chapter, and they must be implemented competently.

A dentist once told me that her area of the city did not have smart people (a statement that is not in line with federal human rights legislation). An office manager said her office was not equipped with the technology needed to ensure a high level of smooth operation, and there was no cash to make such an investment. Such excuses didn't help their practice succeed and won't help yours.

The Three Drivers of a Responsible Practice
1. Hygiene Appointments
2. Future Treatments
3. Accounts Receivable

A dental practice has income and expenses similar to any business. In a dental practice, the two main income channels are patients and insurance companies. It's worth noting that although the patients themselves only contribute around 30 percent of the income, depending on their insurance plans, and the remaining 70 percent comes from insurance. Without patients, there is no insurance portion of the income. The expenses include similar expenses to any other business in terms of debt, interest and principal, rent, utilities, salaries, marketing and advertising, continuous education, equipment leasing, and other regular business expenses. This is a relatively simplistic way of describing a business, but those are the main components a dental practice shares with other businesses. It's important to keep these components simple so everyone can grasp them.

In Canada, most people have some sort of private insurance coverage, paid partly by the employee and partly by the employer. In addition to dental benefits, it includes prescription glasses, massages, and discounts on select medications. Most plans cover 80 percent of the cost of any basic dental treatment, such as extractions and fillings.

They cover 50 percent of all major treatments, such as surgical extractions and root canals. The percentage covered can vary from plan to plan. In general terms, as mentioned earlier, 70 percent of the income of an average dental practice comes from insurance companies and 30 percent from patients. Dental associations offer a fee guide and, together with the insurance companies, are able to determine which procedure is minor and which procedure is major. They also suggest the fee amount for each procedure.

Income, therefore, is determined by the number of patients and the office's ability to track these payments, which is the third of the three drivers that need to be managed efficiently if the dental practice is to be successful. We looked at these drivers briefly in Chapters 1 and 2. Let us look at each of these drivers in turn.

1. HYGIENE APPOINTMENTS

The first driver in a dental practice consists of hygiene cleaning appointments. There is general consensus among dentists and insurance companies that the average human being needs two professional teeth cleanings per year for better oral health. This regime also contributes to a lower chance of oral cancer and reduced decay and gum disease.[2]

Despite this consensus, it always surprises me that dental offices struggle to consistently bring patients in twice a year for a cleaning. This is even more astounding considering most Canadians have insurance that covers 80 percent of those biannual appointments. It should be very easy for dental offices to draw their patients' attention

---

2   Luzia A. Marques et al., "Oral Health, Hygiene Practices and Oral Cancer," *Revista de Saúda Pública* 42, no. 3 (2008): 471-479.

to available research showing that cleanings lower the risk of oral disease, yet patients are still not coming twice a year for cleanings.

A fundamental rule for a successful dental practice is to routinely schedule the next hygiene appointment for each patient. This strategy is the bare minimum that needs to be done if you want to have a successful and busy dental practice. A hygiene cleaning appointment is usually at a lower cost to the patient, and therefore lower revenue for the practice, but the volume is higher than dental procedures. At the end of each hygiene appointment, the dentist should examine the patient's teeth. Problems should be diagnosed and a treatment plan created to take care of gaps in the patient's oral health.

There are three ways to ensure this key service is managed properly. First, while the patient is in the chair, whether it's at the end of a teeth-cleaning appointment or at the end of another procedure, the treatment provider needs to book the next cleaning appointment six months in advance, *before* the patient leaves. Teeth cleanings should be booked regardless of whether a patient has an appointment scheduled for another procedure—for example, a filing scheduled for three weeks later. Many clinics say that if the patient has an appointment for an upcoming treatment, it's not necessary to make a future hygiene appointment because the patient is going to come back to the clinic anyway. This is a mistake, as the appointment could be overlooked on any given visit. As a rule of thumb, when one hygiene appointment is finished, make sure the next is in the calendar. The importance of this hygiene cleaning appointment should be stressed to the patient.

The second way is to ensure that you have the right tools and

As a rule of thumb, when one hygiene appointment is finished, make sure the next is in the calendar.

processes in place to remind the patient about the future appointment. Since it's booked six months in advance, the chances of the patient remembering it are slim. This means your office needs to have a system in place to make sure the patient is reminded of that upcoming appointment. The frequency of those reminders depends on whether they are done by phone, e-mail, text, or regular mail. Your choice of communication method depends both on the nature of your patients and on what tools are available to you as a practice owner. Usually, multiple reminders sent at different times are most effective.

For some offices, it makes sense to send a reminder a month in advance, then a week in advance, and then about three days before that particular appointment. Some offices go the extra mile of calling patients on the morning of their appointment just to make sure they are coming, even if they confirmed via text, e-mail, or over the phone.

The third action that contributes to ensuring every patient has cleaning appointments booked is giving staff access to the patient database to check for those who don't have a hygiene appointment booked. Creating a process for staff to work on that list daily to ensure it is empty is advisable.

In addition to health and prophylactic benefits, having a future hygiene appointment scheduled for all of your patients has the benefit of predictable income for the hygiene department.

From a business standpoint, another reason for the importance of hygiene appointments is that they generate repeat business. The dentist can assess the patient's oral health needs at the end of a hygiene appointment and recommend future treatment if needed. If any work needs to be done, it should be logged and tracked, which brings us to the second driver.

2. FUTURE TREATMENTS

The second of the three drivers of a dental practice is future treatment, which can occur when there is a walk-in emergency, when new patients come in, or when a dentist diagnoses treatment based on a checkup after the hygiene appointment. Walk-in emergencies happen frequently; many patients just walk in the door in serious pain and need to see a dentist.

Obviously, an emergency would take precedence over the other two conditions, but a dentist should also do a general exam of the entire mouth to diagnose any other problems a patient might have. When performing exams, there is opportunity to enhance the relationship by conversing with the patients, learning more about their lifestyle and sharing information about yours. Providing good oral health advice is also recommended and usually appreciated. Whether the patient needs additional treatment or not, checkups offer an opportunity to forge a relationship between dentist and patient or enhance the existing one.

Although new patients and walk-in emergencies do contribute to diagnosed dental conditions and future treatments, it is existing dental patients who account for most treatments, as there are usually more existing patients than walk-ins (unless it's a fairly new practice). These existing patients hold the dentist accountable for their oral health. They rely on the dentists, staff, and their processes and tools to take care of their oral health.

> **Although new patients and walk-in emergencies do contribute to diagnosed dental conditions and future treatments, it is existing dental patients who account for most treatments.**

It is important to stress that dental work should never be diagnosed and performed unnecessarily for the sake of bringing in revenue. This is a worrying trend shared by large groups of dentists in Canada. I do not recommend performing unnecessary treatment. As a dentist, it is your responsibility (and your oath) to provide the best advice and treatment for your patients. Do not do unnecessary treatments for the sake of bringing money to your clinic. This will not foster a long-term relationship with your patient or help your reputation. There are other, more ethical ways of making money.

Documenting Health Records

One aspect of setting up future appointments involves documenting health records. I am a frequent visitor to two great websites: those of the Royal College of Dental Surgeons of Ontario (RCDSO) and the College of Dental Surgeons of British Columbia (CDSBC). Following these two organizations allows me to understand regulations and stay abreast of emerging issues and areas of importance for the industry.

A recurring problem listed on these sites is failure to properly document health records. In a similar process to that of privacy investigations, regulators turn to the patient's health records when investigating a complaint.

Do an exercise. Go to your association's website and look for the summaries of the disciplinary committee. You'll see that regardless of the nature of the complaint, there is a category for failure to properly document the patient's health records.

When performing an exam, you are obligated to document your findings and your discussion with the patient. Different treatments, and their pros and cons, should be discussed and listed. The treatment you recommend should be discussed, justified, and documented.

Many dentists only recommend one treatment and ask their patients to schedule an appointment. They don't explain the condition, options for treatment, risks, or pros and cons. This sends shivers down my spine. These dentists say that there is not enough time for all of these collateral activities because they have quotas, goals, billing-per-hour metrics, and two patients waiting in operatories. There is no time to chit chat with patients.

However, discussing and documenting the patient's treatment, options, risks, and potential side effects do not only provide exceptional service but is the standard for providing oral health services. Educating patients will lead them to recognize their dentist as a professional upon whom they can rely.

This internal process is handled differently across practices. Some dental clinics have software to create digital charts, but some are still using paper charts. This means that staff members need to make sure that the diagnosed treatment specified on the paper chart is entered into the patient management software as a future treatment so that the practice can track which patients require treatment and when.

For example, in most practices, behind the receptionist is a bookcase with all the paper charts in a colorful array of folders that include medical questionnaires and other support documents. Staff members will need to schedule the diagnosed treatment for the patients who require it but will have no idea which folders belong to patients requiring future treatment. They have to look through a shelf of charts unless future treatments are entered into the database system every time a paper chart travels from the operatory, where it was filled out by the dentist, to their desk. Whatever software is being used must have the ability to show which patients need treatment, help coordinate insurance approvals, and schedule treatments.

If you already use digital charts, the necessary data is generated in the operatory and synchronised with the patient database. This saves the front staff from having to re-enter the information from the paper chart into the database. It also reduces the human error that may occur when a staff member has to interpret handwriting when entering the information into the electronic health record system.

Once information is entered into your digital system, staff members must have processes in place to make sure that these treatments are transformed into appointments.

Another advantage to proper documentation arises when dealing with a malicious patient. There are times when you do everything right, but the patient goes to another practitioner, who provides alternative diagnosis. This is an opportunity for malicious patients to file a complaint against you. You are going to have to answer to your regulatory body, and in the case of poor documentation, pay fines of anywhere from $2000 to $30,000. You may be forced to take courses in ethics and record keeping at your own expense. You may incur negative public exposure and even suffer a temporary revocation of your license.

However, properly maintained records can serve as evidence of your work, actions, and reasons for your recommendations. In other words, health records are your insurance policy against potential fraudulent claims made against you to the regulatory bodies.

Case Acceptance

The term "case acceptance" describes the process and ability of the staff to ensure the patient accepts the suggested future treatment and undergoes the treatment.

Because the patients rely on the clinic's staff and processes to uphold proper oral health, it's not enough for the dentist to just diagnose and prescribe a treatment plan. This is essential, but without the proper tracking and without ensuring that the patients are following through on their proposed treatment plan, dentists will fail in their responsibility as medical practitioners.

The question now becomes how to get patients to accept the proposed treatment and show up for their appointments, especially if they have to pay hundreds or thousands of dollars in costs that are not covered by their insurance company. How can you, the dental owner, make sure that at the end of their treatment, your patients still love your practice and recommend it to friends and family?

Case acceptance, or buy-in, is another way to ensure that diagnosed treatment becomes an appointment. Basically, this means that patients, especially those undergoing major treatment, of which the insurance covers only 50 percent, may not accept their treatment plan because of the cost to them. If they had to pay zero, they would accept the treatment. What you are facing, as a dental owner, is getting patients who have to foot a large bill to say, "Yes, it costs a lot of money, but I believe I really need to do this."

A dentist's medical authority is not enough to ensure that patients move ahead with an expensive treatment. In a dental practice, case acceptance comes from establishing a deep and meaningful relationship with the patient. But how do you foster this kind of relationship? First, you must *want* to establish it. If you don't want to and you just think of the patient-dentist relationships as something you have to do because it's your job, it likely won't work. For dentists, who are usually introverts, this is a major challenge. Introverted dentists must step out of their comfort zone and learn to enjoy social interaction.

If you choose to provide a service to people, you must get a handle on your introversion. If you see social interaction as a chore, you should not pursue a service profession. Providing service to people requires, at the very minimum, interaction and rapport. Unfortunately, many dentists consider patient interaction to be a necessary evil. This is a problem for a dental practice because social interaction is one of the biggest parameters affecting patient buy-in. The social interaction leverages the patient-doctor relationship so the patient can say, "This dentist is not just a doctor. He cares about me. He would never recommend a treatment just to get money from me. If he says I need it, then I must need it."

The key to persuading patients to follow through on treatment is properly explaining why they need the treatment and the repercussions of not undergoing it. Dentists are not only sharing information but explaining it in a way that shows they're trying to look after the best interest of the patient. Information and explanation increase the authority of the dentist and instill in the patient a sense of confidence in the professionalism and competence of the dentist.

One tool, which we'll talk about in Chapter 8, is taking pictures of the patient's mouth. It contributes to patient buy-in because the dentist can illustrate what needs to happen. This also allows for a before-and-after comparison.

Insurance Approvals and Tracking

Once a treatment is recommended, particularly a major treatment, it is important to have a system to track insurance company pre-authorizations for major treatment. This necessitates an open line of communication with insurance companies and proper tracking tools.

If you don't have a system in place to track insurance approvals, nothing will happen after a treatment is prescribed until the patient calls your clinic to follow up. This is a reactive approach that contributes to a less efficient practice and a less than full schedule for the doctor. Additionally, since insurance approvals are sent to the patients, the patients are empowered to choose their service provider more freely. Without the proper follow-up, the patient may go to another clinic to undergo the treatment.

I often encounter offices that are struggling because they don't have an efficient tracking system to follow up on everything they send for approval. The practice needs a system that allows its staff to stay on top of approvals. The office needs to call patients and ask if they got the approval from their insurance company.

If you have a patient management system, you know that three to five days after the recommended treatment, the patient will get a letter in the mail telling them if they've been approved. Your system needs to be set up so that it knows when to call the patient to say, "Hello, did you receive approval from the insurance company? We'd like to follow up and book the treatment you need." If you don't have that system, not all the treatments will be booked.

If the preauthorization is denied, the patient faces many obstacles to committing to the treatment. If their condition is urgent, however, they might decide to fight their insurance company later on.

Once you have a proper system in place to track those insurance approvals, you have to get the patient to come in for the treatment, which becomes an internal, or staff, process. Having a software system is the first step, but the staff must use the system and have a process for calling, e-mailing, and/or texting patients to follow up on the preauthorization approval and book the appointment for the treatment. Your internal staffing structure or process should determine who is responsible for calling and what their measurable goal is.

3. ACCOUNTS RECEIVABLE

The biggest portion of income in your dental practice comes from insurance companies. From a cash flow perspective, it's important to have a system in place to make sure that you know which income comes from which insurance company and when it can be expected. Tracking accounts receivable, therefore, is crucial to cash-flow health and thus the success of the practice.

This particular driver is closely connected with the way that the owner of the clinic pays associate dentists. There are different ways to pay associates, but whichever system is used, it must correlate with the income coming to the practice. We will look at this in more depth in Chapter 8 when we explore remuneration structures.

Non-Assignable Offices

A non-assignable office is one that charges patients in full for their treatments. Their patients must come up with the full amount for all dental procedures and fight with their insurers for reimbursement. These practices therefore enjoy zero dealings with insurance companies.

Since these practices only deal with patient accounts receivable, accounts have to be written off if patients can't pay or don't meet the payment plan. One way to offset this risk is by having an arrangement with a financial establishment with which the patients can work. The clinic therefore gets the payment in full after the treatment is completed, while the patient makes monthly payments to the financial establishment.

Assignable Offices

Assignable offices take a portion of the payment from patients, which is based on their insurance policy, and submit a claim to the insurance company for the rest of the payment. This creates a situation where both insurance and patient accounts receivable must be collected. In this situation, the majority of the cash flow comes from insurance companies. In my experience, insurance companies try their best to pay as little as possible as late as possible. This is the way they protect their assets (since cash generates interest for them daily), monitor for fraud, and ensure accuracy of claims. Do not be surprised or put off by their practices, as this is a legitimate business technique in the world of insurance. Instead, make certain you have a system and a process in place to ensure that you are collecting what you are due in a timely manner. When you and your team know at any given time what you are owed (from patient or insurance company) and when you can expect payment, you will have a sense of control over your cash flow. This knowledge contributes immensely to the stability and reduced stress of a dental clinic.

THE RECIPE FOR SUCCESS

The recipe for success in a dental practice is based on efficiently and effectively implementing these three drivers. To be successful, you need to implement and synergize these drivers. Having all three in place turns your practice into a well-oiled machine.

If you're able to properly manage the first driver (hygiene cleaning appointments), you will find that your hygienists are fully booked far in advance. This is the minimum of where you want to be. If you're starting to book hygiene appointments and you're fully booked two months in advance, that means you have either too few hygienists or too many patients, so you need to grow your physical facility, employ more hygienists, or extend your hours.

Having your hygienists booked solid for two or three weeks is a good indication that you're on top of hygiene cleaning appointments for your active patients.

The same principle applies to future treatments, but this involves the dentists in the practice, not the hygienists. If there's a proper tracking system and process for booking the pre-scribed future treatments, you'll be able to see all of your dentists solidly booked for two or three weeks a month. Depending on the number of dentists, the number of patients, and the physical facility, it might be necessary to grow by adding more dentists or opening another location.

Having your hygienists booked solid for two or three weeks is a good indication that you're on top of hygiene cleaning appointments for your active patients.

The third driver—staying on top of your accounts receivable—gives you an awareness of how much income is coming in and when. You can quickly see if there's a problem with the insurance companies that you need to tackle. It also informs you of when you will be paid for work you did two weeks earlier and assures you that you are getting paid for work rendered. Knowing what income is coming, where is it coming from, and when gives you a sense of control. With these drivers in place, you have laid the groundwork and can continue to build on your success.

WHAT MATTERS MOST

I remember wrapping up to go home late one Friday evening in our office in Winnipeg, when the phone rang. It was Dr. Rashford, and she was livid. She spent the first ten minutes of the conversation screaming at me about how her production had been dropping substantially in the two years they had been using our software. In servicing thousands of dentists, I hear plenty of complaints, but a reduction in production has never been one of them.

I looked up her file and saw an obvious issue. At the time of change/purchase, in order to save money, she opted out of the recommended three-day, on-site implementation process and only had four hours of online training for her staff of eight. I also realized her frustration was mainly due to the dental providers, including herself, being less busy with patients. I asked about her processes for managing the diagnosed/future treatments and discovered a huge hole: they switched software about the same time the insurance companies started sending insurance approvals to patients instead of clinics, but Dr. Rashford's processes did not include a proactive approach to follow up on these insurance approvals.

I showed her their aged future treatment report and she was blown away by the number of recommended treatments they had not followed up on and therefore did not book. When patients came back for their next hygiene appointment, the dentist had to diagnose again and ensure there hadn't been any change in the condition that would necessitate a different type of treatment, which would require another insurance approval.

Dr. Rashford discovered, as they started reaching out to patients needing treatment, that 50 percent of them had the treatment performed at a different clinic. This was a huge blow.

Over the next few months, I was able to guide Dr. Rashford's team to properly track future treatments, including managing the insurance approvals and modifying their existing processes to minimize the risk of patients going to other clinics or opting to not treat their condition. Her team was then able to ensure proper booking and treatment of their patients.

Soon both dental providers at Dr. Rashford's practice became booked thirty days in advance and had a problem accommodating urgent treatments and emergencies. She had to expand her facility to create another operatory and hire another associate. That's a good problem to have compared to not having enough appointments booked.

This story shows the need to be proactive, have processes for everything, and not be solely dependent on third parties to trigger events in your practice. At the end of the day, you need to devise processes and workflows so that you have control over all three drivers in your dental practice.

The next area that needs your attention is HR and expanding the trust and respect you've established with your office manager and patients to the rest of your staff. We'll look at this more in the next chapter.

CHAPTER 4

HUMAN RESOURCES: INTERPERSONAL ISSUES

Dealing with interpersonal issues in any practice can be a source of great stress. My initial encounter with extreme stress came when I had to fire an employee for the first time. I was twenty-three years old, and the employee was fifty-four. I was fairly new to the job, while he had been there for over twelve years. To make matters worse, it was peak season, and I had no one to take his place.

I had given the employee some warnings, and with each warning my stress grew. I couldn't sleep for three days. I was tormented by the impact on people's lives that I could have as a manager. I couldn't shake the thought of my actions changing a person's life. Eventually, it became evident that the employee was not going to change. I knew that he had brought it upon himself and that I was just doing my job. However, I was completely stressed by the time I met with the employee and informed him of his termination. It was awkward, and it took me another two months to get over the feeling of disgust and contempt I felt for myself.

That situation taught me that stress comes from doing something we don't want to do or something we don't believe in, combined with inexperience or lack of knowledge. It impacts our well-being and can cause depression and a mental or physical breakdown.

There are very few jobs with zero stress. Stress is part of life in our modern world. This means it is important to be in a place where you love what you do and focus on your purpose. This is the most effective way to minimize stress and wake up happier.

STRESS AND HUMAN RESOURCES

Handling HR can be very stressful for a dental owner and office manager. However, with some knowledge and tools, you can learn to manage this area and your stress.

There are two main elements to consider when dealing with HR. The first is the technical element—that is, skills that are easy to acquire through experience, similar to reading body language, reading resumes, writing job ads, interviewing, even some HR coaching and mentoring. We will return to this aspect of running a business in the next chapter.

Another element that is more intangible or holistic than the ability to read a resume is the ability to find the right people. One of the most common complaints I hear from dentists and dental office managers is that they can't find competent staff. This comes from a lack of leadership and clear direction, a lack of understanding of what needs to be done in the dental practice and how it needs to be run, and the inability of leadership to clearly communicate these responsibilities to staff. The lack of specialized training to work in a dental environment is also a contributing factor to this problem.

Recently, my dental association conducted a survey of dental practices and found that staff turnover is another big challenge for dentists and dental office managers. High turnover rate is another side effect of not

> **One of the most common complaints I hear from dentists and dental office managers is that they can't find competent staff.**

having clarity of purpose and an ability to communicate expectations. Without these, employees end up not knowing what they should be doing, how they should be doing it, what goals they need to achieve, and how they fit in the organization. Because expectations are not being communicated, the dentist and/or office manager can have one perception or set of expectations and the employees can have another, which creates a lot of conflict.

A high turnover of employees suggests a high level of stress, which indicates there are HR problems that need to be addressed.

The majority of human behavior is emotionally driven, and a higher percentage is driven by negative emotions. The world is buzzing about stress—specifically, work-related stress. It is making people sick. In this section, we will focus on the stressors relevant to dental clinics.

> **A high turnover of employees suggests a high level of stress, which indicates there are HR problems that need to be addressed.**

Stressors can be divided into two groups: organizational and personal.

There are three main causes of organizational stress in a dental practice: ambiguity, organizational leadership, and interpersonal demands. In our survey, we didn't always find all three present, but these three were the most common experiences shared by partici-pants. In all of the interviews I conducted with dental practice employees, I was told stories that vividly illustrated these stressors as a reason for their wish to leave their position or even industry.

The three main organiz-tion stressors:

Ambiguity
Organizational Leadership
Interpersonal Demands

ORGANIZATIONAL STRESSORS

Ambiguity

Ambiguity is a very powerful stressor that occurs when employees do not know what their job entails, what is expected of them, and what their contribution to the clinic should be, its purposes, or goals.

The impact of ambiguity of office functionality and morale is one of the reasons it was so important to clearly define the purpose of the practice and communicate that to staff. Not only does it help in day-to-day decision making, but it also helps the employees achieve what's called line of sight—that is, the connection between their daily tasks and the goals, vision, and purpose of the clinic. This connection is key to building their awareness that they are a part of something bigger than themselves, which, most importantly, gives them purpose. This is especially true of the millennial generation.

Purpose is essential to their happiness and retention. One of the most important things to millennials (in a work environment setting) is line of sight, which allows them to adopt the company's goals as their own. This is why ambiguity is problematic and clarity and purpose are connected. Remember that purpose always starts with the person who leads the practice, the person who determines why the practice is open for business. In a dental clinic, this role

> **Purpose always starts with the person who leads the practice**

generally falls to the dental owner. In a perfect world, it would fall to the dental owner in collaboration with the dental office manager.

Organizational Leadership

Organizational leadership relates to the style of management of the dental owner, especially if there is no dental office manager. Even if there is a dental office manager, how dentists carry themselves and how they work with the dental office manager affects the staff, their perceptions of how they should behave, and how much respect they give the office manager.

The style and nature of middle management and how these managers carry themselves will affect how much stress they cause employees and, in turn, employees' perception of them. For example, a people pleaser is a type of manager who goes to extremes to build close, personal, and friendly relationships with staff. However, going to work is not about making new friends; it is about getting work done and achieving goals. Making new friends can be a by-product of good work and should never be the actual goal.

Another type of manager is the egoistical manager. These managers care more about their own success than that of the company.

They will run over their employees on their way to making their quota. In bigger practices, there may be multiple treatment coordinators, one of whom is the senior or team leader, who works with the office managers on additional tasks and speaks for the team. Their style and agenda is instrumental in how their team responds to them.

Being a manager means empowering team members to realize their potential to grow and learn. The manager should inspire them to think outside the box and push them outside their comfort zone to find better ways to achieve their goals.

Stress is good up to a certain degree, but it's important to not overdo it. The higher the stress, the lower the job satisfaction. It's important to make sure that the management style adopted in your practice is consistent with the purpose and the goals of the practice.

> **Stress is good up to a certain degree, but it's important to not overdo it. The higher the stress, the lower the job satisfaction.**

Interpersonal Demands

Interpersonal stressors created by coworkers—for example, lack of collaboration, poor collaboration, low trust, and poor teamwork—cause a lot of stress for employees because they feel they are alone. Even if there is a bigger goal to achieve, they feel it will never be achieved because they are the only ones working hard, or at least working harder than anyone else. They feel the goal is not achievable, so the purpose becomes irrelevant and everything collapses.

It is interesting to note that the bigger the clinic, the more interpersonal connections may be, so this particular type of stressor may be much greater.

PERSONAL STRESSORS

There are two main personal stressors for employees: lifestyle and finances.

Lifestyle

Lifestyle stressors may include divorce, aging parents, marriage, a new child, or children misbehaving at school. While these stressors are part of your home life and not your professional life, you can't check them at the door. As such, they can affect relationships with coworkers, bosses, and even patients.

Lifestyle stressors are very difficult to avoid because they're not part of what dental owners or office managers can control. Employees might not even see the impact on their work, patients, or coworkers. However, having a good and solid relationship with employees will allow them to open up and share their difficulties. If they feel comfortable sharing with the office manager the details of difficult lifestyle circumstances, their stressors can be overcome. However, if an employee continues to let personal problems affect patients, the office manager must take drastic measures to see that the reputations of the clinic and the dentist are not affected.

The dental owner and the office manager should want a practice where everyone is happy. There should be good customer service, happy patients, revenue, and a growing practice. However, the reality is mixed. All staff members bring their own baggage and personal life into the practice. Sometimes, life doesn't go the way we want, but it's important that personal issues are identified and addressed to prevent affecting the clinic.

Financial

One of the reasons dentists spend their whole day in the operatory is because they feel the weight of that debt, and they know that they have to produce to pay it off.

Financial stressors, such as credit card debt and gambling, can be stressors if they exceed income. A dental owner usually carries hundreds of thousands of dollars in debt. One of the reasons dentists spend their whole day in the operatory is because they feel the weight of that debt, and they know that they have to produce to pay it off.

If dental practice employees, who have a fixed income, are not smart about their money and instead accumulate huge credit card debt or have a gambling or other financial problem, they pose a danger not only to themselves but also to the dental owner. Financial stressors lead to embezzlement or even attempts to blackmail the dentist. It is not unheard of for a stressed employee, aware of patient privacy regulations, to obtain a copy of health records and try to blackmail the dentist: "Look, I'm going to expose this and breach your confidentiality. I'm going to destroy your reputation unless …" Some people embezzle because that's their nature, but a good employee who starts to embezzle after working for fifteen years in a dental practice may have personal financial problems, perhaps as a result of drinking, gambling, or other financial commitments made outside the business.

If the origin of an employee's stress is financial, immediate attention is required. As with lifestyle stressors, fostering a good relationship with your employees will create an environment where they feel comfortable in sharing their problems. Most organizational stressors can be prevented, or at least mitigated, by defining the practice's purpose, ensuring clear communication, holding frequent meetings, and setting expectations. While personal stressors can't be prevented by the dental owner, it is important to address them when they become apparent so they don't become worse.

PASSIVE AND ACTIVE METHODS FOR DEALING WITH STRESS

Dealing with stress is an acquired skill. There are five main ways of dealing with stress: two passive and three active. It's important to not only know about these methods but also practice dealing with stress constantly and consistently. All staff members need to be aware of these methods so they're able to use them as stressful situations arise.

Dealing with stress is an acquired skill.

Passive methods of handling stress involve perception. As Mark Twain said, "I've had a lot of worries in my life, most of which never happened." Many times, our perception of a situation was worse than the event itself. The more familiar the situation is to us, the more likely we are to have this passive ability to shift our perception to relieve our stress.

Job experience is another passive method for relieving stress. The more job experience you have, the more you feel able to deal with a stressful situation because either you dealt with a similar problem earlier or you have gained the knowledge to deal with it.

Active methods give you some control over stressors and stress relief. Active methods include taking care of yourself through physical exercise, relaxation, and diet and nutrition.

Physical activity has been known as a stress reliever for quite a while now. On top of the release of aggression, it contributes to weight control, which has other physiological effects on the body in terms of high blood pressure and joint pain.[3]

When you are interviewing candidates, ask them how they deal with stress or what they do for stress relief. Working with patients all day is stressful, regardless of whether you are a receptionist, dental assistant, hygienist, or dentist. All employees must have their own way of coping with stress.

From the thousands of interviews I've conducted, I've found the most popular among stress-relieving activities are reading, music, exercise, and computer games, but it's very important for all staff members to have the ability to explain how they deal with accumulated stress during and after work.

Relaxation comes from scheduled free time and an annual vacation. In both cases, the mind is free from thoughts of work. These periods don't necessarily coincide with a stressful period in the employee's day, but knowing that they are soon to go on vacation can bring stress relief to employees.

Immediate relaxation is an activity that the individual can practice when a stressful situation occurs. It may involve a short break for meditation, having some tea, or taking a walk. It's an efficient way of dealing with stress in the moment.

Employees repeatedly taking walks around the building may be a red flag to the dental owner or office manager that they are out of their comfort zone and are getting stressed easily. It is very important

3   Rebecca Rueggeberg, Carsten Wrosch, and Gregory E. Miller, "The Different Reults of Perceived Stress in the Association between Older Adults' Physical Activity and Physical Health," *Health Psychol* 31, no. 2 (2012): 164–171.

this is addressed because it means these employees' skill sets and strengths may not be in line with the position they hold.

Diet and nutrition are important in active stress management. They say that we are what we eat. High fat content and sugary foods stimulate and prolong the alarm state in stressful situations.[4] We don't want to prolong a state of alarm, especially when dealing with stress. Therefore, having a healthy diet contributes to the ability of the body, not only emotionally but also physically, to deal with stress more efficiently.

EQUITY THEORY AND OFFICE FAIRNESS

The term *equity theory* relates to how human beings—or in the dental clinic context, employees—perceive equity, or fairness. People subconsciously interpret different interactions with their peers and with their bosses. Dental owners and managers can do little to change this process precisely because it is a subconscious, automatic reaction. However, they should be aware it happens, because they're interacting with their employees all day.

---

4   Walid El Ansari, Sakari Suominen, and Gabriele Berg-Beckhoff, "Mood and Food at the University of Turku in Finland: Nutritional Correlates of Percieved Stress Are Most Pronounced among Overweight Students," *International Journal of Public* Health 60 (2015): 707–716.

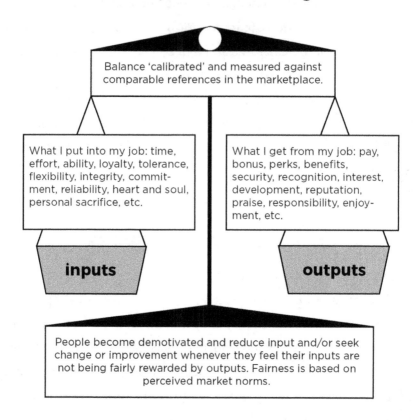

Adam's EQUITY THEORY diagram

Balance 'calibrated' and measured against comparable references in the marketplace.

What I put into my job: time, effort, ability, loyalty, tolerance, flexibility, integrity, commitment, reliability, heart and soul, personal sacrifice, etc.

What I get from my job: pay, bonus, perks, benefits, security, recognition, interest, development, reputation, praise, responsibility, enjoyment, etc.

inputs

outputs

People become demotivated and reduce input and/or seek change or improvement whenever they feel their inputs are not being fairly rewarded by outputs. Fairness is based on perceived market norms.

Figure 4.1. *An individual equity diagram measured against the perceived diagram of a colleague. The perceived ratio is then put to the test of which is greater.*[5]

For example, individuals measure their perceived reward against their perceived efforts in comparison with their perception of a peer's reward measured against that peer's efforts. This affects the dental practice in a number of ways, notably remuneration structure.

For example, a dentist once told me that in order to avoid misperceptions, his clinic implemented a group bonus for achieving the clinic's goals. When the clinic's goals were achieved, all employees got

---

5   J. Kandpal, "Equity Theory of Motivation," *Slideshare*, 2015, https://www.slide-share.net/JyotiKandpal2/equity-theory-of-motivation-53432579.

the same bonus. On the surface, this looks like an optimal solution, but from a perceived fairness perspective, one employee may believe he or she contributed more than another employee to the overall clinical goal and therefore perceives the bonus as unfair because it was the same as everyone else's.

However, when you give employees control over the metric and provide them with a bonus for meeting it, they perceive the bonus as fair. Therefore, if they perceive they have control, but they do not achieve their goal, it is more difficult for them to view the lack of a bonus as unfair or to blame other people. It can be an individual or a team goal, but as long as employees perceive they have control over their actions and the outcome, it works. Finding a solution to the perception of fairness, or equity, depends on the people, practice, processes, and goals. Ideally, all employees in the dental clinic should be responsible for their own metric and should therefore be remunerated on this metric only.

The biggest impact can be seen in decisions taken on a remuneration structure or a bonus structure. Not everyone will interpret the decisions of the operations manager, the dental office manager, or the dentist in the same way. This is a good example of why clear metrics in the dental practice are key to preventing mistakes in the interpretation of equity.

Clear metrics in the dental practice are key to preventing mistakes in the interpretation of equity.

ORGANIZATIONAL BEHAVIOR

During my MBA studies, I took a course that dealt with organizational behavior, which is directly related to HR. It discussed the difference between introverted and extroverted employees. Introverts enjoy working on their own and avoid social interaction, while extroverts thrive on social interaction.

Recent research[6] shows that the impact of the different groups on individual motivation is actually very low. Introverts and extroverts are equally effective when put in the right position or social environment. More relevant to the dental practice are the concepts of the internalist and the externalist.[7]

Internalists vs. Externalists

Internalists see their efforts as instrumental in achieving a reward or a goal. Externalists perceive that achieving a goal is not dependent on their action but, rather, on a combination of external factors. What this means is that it doesn't matter what they do; external factors determine whether the goal will be achieved or whether the reward is given. Based on those definitions, it's advisable to fill your organization with internalists, but that doesn't mean it's easy to keep them employed, motivated, and happy.

The millennial generation is made up of both internalists and externalists. However, having conducted many interviews with millennials, I've learned that the majority of them are seeking to make a difference, have an impact, and feel fulfilled. This means they will be

6   N. Krimgold, (2002), "Extroversion, Introversion, and the Brain," *Serendip Studio*. Bryn Mawr College, Pennsylvania, available at http://serendip.brynmawr.edu/ biology/b103/f03/web1/nkrimgold.html.

7   "Internalist vs. Externalist Conceptions of Epistemic Justification," *Stanford Encyclopedia of Philosophy*, n.d., available at https://plato.stanford.edu/entries/ justep-intext/.

happy in a practice structured to allow goals. Therefore, if you show them their actions lead to the achievement of a goal or a particular reward, they will continue to be happier and more motivated.

For instance, in a large dental practice, it makes sense to employ what is called a treatment coordinator. Based on what we learned in previous chapters about tracking follow-up treatments, the treatment coordinator uses various tools to ensure everything is tracked: the dental schedule is full, the approvals from the insurance come through, the patients are booked, and the financial structure accommodates the patients' ability to pay for their treatments. Therefore, since responsibilities, expectations, and the ability to interact with others constitutes 80 percent of the job, 80 percent of the job parameters are under the direct control of that individual, who, to be effective, needs access to the necessary information and tools. Make these tools available, along with a clear job description, and a remuneration structure that rewards achievement, and you have created a position that will highly motivate an internalist.

LEADERSHIP AND MENTORING

Real leadership is the dual ability to make sure your team is able to succeed, combined with mentorship to give them the feeling they've succeeded because of their own efforts. This strengthens their self-confidence and allows them to continuously grow and learn because the more their self-confidence grows, the more they believe they can achieve.

Being a leader is only fulfilling if your driver is your desire to see people grow and blossom. If you're playing a leadership/mentorship role because you want to get praise for how great you are, you're not going to be successful. You're going to be miserable.

Coaching and mentoring means guiding people through failures and mistakes. This is the best way to learn and gain experience. If you try to mentor people by telling them exactly what they need to do and making sure they do it, you're not a leader, and you're not a mentor. You are a supervisor, and what you're doing is ensuring processes are followed. There's no creativity there. Telling people how to solve a problem limits their professional growth and prevents them from realizing their potential.

> Being a leader is only fulfilling if your driver is your desire to see people grow and blossom. If you're playing a leadership/mentorship role because you want to get praise for how great you are, you're not going to be successful. You're going to be miserable.

This kind of supervision in lieu of proper mentoring leaves no room for exceptional customer service. This is because exceptional customer service only occurs outside the regular process. We'll look at this more in chapter 6.

Most people want (or claim they want) to improve themselves. However, there are many people who choose to behave in the same way regardless of repeated negative outcomes. This is because people are willing to accept a bad outcome rather than face change, or they fear that behaving differently will lead to even worse results.

Dr. Ferguson found this out when he hired a new receptionist. His practice has been steadily growing in the ten years since he opened it. He had, initially, hired Brittany as a receptionist, but as the practice grew, she became the unofficial office manager and, later, the official office manager. Since making her position official, Brittany began to take on fewer responsibilities and became less communicative with the dentist and the rest of the staff members who felt she wasn't pulling her weight. This situation persists today because of fear of the unknown.

1.   The dentist does not replace Brittany. (Mentoring and clarifying expectations are advisable before taking this measure.) He is afraid he will not be able to find anyone better.

2.   Staff members are not happy but are not leaving because they have bills to pay and are afraid they will not find another job. They stay but do mediocre work.

3.   Brittany is not self-aware enough to realize what is happening and make changes.

Self-awareness is crucial. It depends a lot on the individual's maturity level, not necessarily chronological age but, rather, mental maturity. Self-awareness takes daily effort and reflection. Everyone should practice it as it is key to personal growth and mindfulness in daily activities.

An inability to face fear and practice self-awareness made Dr. Ferguson and his practice my biggest failure in terms of turning around a clinic. However, his situation provided me with valuable lessons and experiences. First, I learned to not push solutions on owner/clients who were resistant to change and accept the status quo because if people don't want to find and implement a solution, my effort is bound to be futile.

> **Self-awareness takes daily effort and reflection. Everyone should practice it as it is key to personal growth and mindfulness in daily activities.**

In my experience, dental owners avoid conflict at all costs. However, if you own a business you should be prepared for occasional conflicts and deal with them to ensure your business is on the right track and adheres to your purpose.

WHAT MATTERS MOST

Dealing with interpersonal issues in any practice can be a source of great stress for the dental owner, but with some tools and knowledge, this stress can be managed.

If, like many dentists, you have trouble finding competent staff, look to your leadership style, your ability to communicate job responsibilities and expectations, and your vision and purpose for the practice, which will also help you reduce staff turnover.

You can reduce stress by being unambiguous, showing strong leadership, and recognizing when an employee is showing signs of lifestyle stress. You can find ways to deal with your own stress through healthy living, exercise, and the practice of mindfulness. The rest of your HR needs can be handled with knowledge, techniques, and tools, which we will look at in the next chapter.

CHAPTER 5

HUMAN RESOURCES: TOOLS OF THE TRADE

As discussed in Chapter 4, HR and interpersonal dynamics can be very stressful for a dental owner and office manager. In this chapter, we will look more at the technical elements and tools you can use to manage your HR and support your business. These tools and techniques include hiring staff, assessing resumes, writing job ads, and conducting interviews.

HIRING STAFF

Many offices need to go through the ad creation process on a regular basis when hiring. There are three basic types of ad: creative ads, corporate ads, and emotional ads. The most important part of creating a job ad is to present the company's purpose and the job's connection to it.

The creative ad is a relatively new, mainstream type that relies on a unique combination of curiosity, humor, and innovation. If your dental practice is innovative, this type of ad will attract the right kind of individuals, which will make it easier to gauge their skills in an interview. If they don't have the skills but have the right personality for your practice, it's better to hire them and train them for the skills you require.

Example of a creative ad

They say that you're never fully dressed without a smile, but what's a smile without clean, beautiful teeth to back it up?

At Our Dental Group, we've spent the last fifty years making sure that every one of our patients walks out the door with a smile that could light up a room.

Today, we're one of the largest oral health groups in Canada, with dozens of dentists, hygienists, assistants, technicians, and support staff helping to keep Winnipeg smiling—and we're still growing!

We're seeking a new hygienist who can help us fill a vacancy for up to eighteen months. If you've got a background in dental hygiene and a passion for helping people, we want to hear from you.

Dental Hygienist

Your purpose in this role will be to provide amazing patient service as a member of our team of expert hygienists. Our patients always receive exceptional care, so whether you're helping an uncomfortable patient, or giving parents tips on how to keep kids' teeth in good shape, you'll need great skills in communication and a positive, helpful attitude.

Practically speaking, you will

- perform all stages of hygiene therapy
- note any oral issues/damage and communicate those problems to our dentists
- develop treatment plans/schedules
- prepare hygiene operatories for patients
- instruct patients in proper oral hygiene
- maintain computerized dental records
- take digital radio/photographs
- manage patient expectations/experience

Working at Our Dental Group

This is a part-time, temporary position, up to 18 months, and up to 29 hrs./wk. The successful applicant will have some choice in shifts to suit work/life balance. These shifts will include a combination of days, evenings, and Saturdays.

We offer a competitive salary of $39.36–$42.45/hour, commensurate with experience, as well as a comprehensive benefits package, vacation, and lots of great team-building events.

Because skill building and education are hugely important to us, you will have the best continuing education opportunities in the business and will always be on the cutting edge of the profession.

Qualifications

- previous experience as a hygienist/dental professional
- strong computer skills, including MS Office
- good basic mathematical skills, and knowledge of dental terminology
- license to practice dental hygiene in Manitoba
- CPR certification
- local anesthesia certification

How to Apply

Our online application will give you the option to apply for this role as a complete person, not just a resume. The application will assess your qualifications, personality traits, and workplace preferences, and should take 10 to 15 minutes to complete. After submitting the application, you'll receive an e-mail inviting you to log in and view your assessment results.

We value diversity and inclusion and encourage all qualified people to apply. If we can make the recruitment process easier, please contact us with the Help button in the application.

We will review applications as they are received and look forward to hearing from you.

The second type of ad is a corporate ad. It's a dry and descriptive outline of the job duties, activities, and responsibilities. It provides candidates with clarification of the skills that are needed for that particular job. Although the applicants might be a good fit in terms of skill, it's going to be very difficult in the interview process to gauge their social fit and mindset and see whether it matches the practice. This is possible in the interview process, but it's more difficult.

Example of a corporate ad

Position: Dentist

Job Posting no: 2016-61

Date: November 17, 2016

Closing Date: Open until filled

Status: Part-time, permanent

Department: Primary Health

Reports to: Primary Health Manager

Hours of Work: Tues. 8:45 a.m.–5 p.m.

Position Description:

Under the leadership, direction and supervision of the Primary Health Manager, the incumbent of this position is responsible for providing dental treatment as outlined by the Manitoba Dental Association.

Qualifications

- licensed to practice dentistry in the Province of Manitoba
- continuing education levels according to Manitoba Dental Association requirements
- CPR certification at the Basic Rescuer Level

- two years related experience; experience in a community care setting preferred
- supervisory experience of dental assistants, dental nurse/therapist, and hygienists performing extra and intra oral treatment procedures
- two years of experience in formulating treatment plans for individual patients and performing clinical treatment
- proficient in electronic clinical documentation
- excellent interpersonal, organizational and communication skills (written and verbal)
- ability to communicate effectively with the public and give clear treatment planning where language and other socio-cultural factors may present challenges
- knowledge and understanding of inner city communities
- knowledge and understanding of indigenous cultures and traditions
- ability to work independently within an inter-disciplinary environment with respect, professionalism, cooperation, sensitivity and cultural skills
- ability to work within the impacts of the social determinants of health in an effective and non-judgmental way
- ability to work in a pro-choice community health facility in an inner-city community and provide care using harm reduction principles
- knowledge of the legacy of residential schools, colonization, assimilation, and the impacts of such history on the health of individuals

- understanding of how culture and diversity influence the client service plan
- ability to mentor, support, and work alongside students and volunteers
- ability to demonstrate acceptable attendance and job performance relevant to this position
- ability to adhere to the requirements of the Respectful Workplace Policy

Applicants may be required to undergo testing to determine their knowledge, skill and ability. All positions are subject to a Criminal Record and Child Abuse Registry check in accordance with Security Checks Policy and Procedures.

Our clinic has undertaken to increase responsiveness to indigenous people by promoting a workforce that is representative of its participant population. Applicants are encouraged to self-declare in their cover letter or resume.

The third type is the emotional ad. To an extent, it's a combination of the two other types. It's the worst ad that you can create, but it's the most often used by dental practices. These ads often reflect the emotional state of the writer. For example, if you had to release an employee or an employee has resigned and you're in a race to quickly find a replacement, you may create this kind of ad. There would be a vague description of the actual tasks and a fairly large amount of personal traits demanded. These are the traits the ad creator perceives were not present in the individual they just released. The ad creator lets emotion write the ad. This is a bad way of going about creating a hiring ad.

Example of an emotional ad

Registered Dental Assistant

Registered dental assistant with orthodontic module required for an established orthodontic practice, 3 to 4 days per week. Position open due to departure of current assistant. Orthodontic experience is preferred, but we are willing to train the right motivated person. No evenings or weekends. The successful candidate will be able to work in a stressful environment with a smile. Please submit resume online. Prospective candidates will be contacted for an interview.

Job Type: Part-time

Required license or certification: Registered Dental Assistant with Orthodontic Module

Tip 1: As your ads run, gauge their effectiveness, which may depend on the location of the practice and the availability of professionals in your region, as will the number of responses to the ad.

Tip 2: Post ads on a Friday morning or afternoon. Most job seekers focus their job seeking efforts throughout the weekend when they're not working.

How to Read a Resume

For most positions, submitting a resume and a cover letter is standard practice. There are two main types of cover letters. The first is written from scratch and matches the candidate's experience to each require-ment in the ad. These candidates excel in writing cover letters and usually describe how they would positively impact your practice. You should want to meet this person based on the cover letter.

The other type of cover letter describes the candidate's personal traits and the experience and skills the candidate believes would be a fit for your position. It is probably used for all of the candidate's job applications.

The candidate's resume needs to fit the position advertised. It should consist of some basic contact information, a summary of qualifications that are relevant to the job, relevant experience, and education. You should make sure there are no gaps in employment. Take note of education, certification, licenses, references, and contact information. References are an easy way for you to verify both experi-ence and skills. If you see that a candidate worked for a colleague, call that colleague regardless of whether he or she is listed as a reference.

The dental industry is relatively small (there are fewer than 30,000 dentists in Canada), so most job seekers will have worked in another dental practice. Because it's a very small community, checking, calling, speaking with or obtaining the candidate's refer-ences allows you reach out to colleagues to ensure these employees left on good terms. If someone doesn't list references, there may be a problem. In fact, a seasoned office manager told me recently that some dental staff members were sending their resumes out with his name as the reference and had a person pretending to be him answer the phone and vouch for them.

When you see a resume that fits the position advertised and includes the pertinent information noted above, you will have a good gauge of the candidate's ability to perform the work required. It doesn't mean you should throw away all the resumes that are written or formatted differently, but make sure you don't accept candidates who submit sloppy resumes, which indicate an inability to take work seriously and maintain focus.

Tip: Sometimes, people send resumes that don't have 100 percent of what you want to see, but those people could have a positive impact on your practice. Remember that behind all resumes are people who may change your practice, and you may change their life.

What to Ask in a Phone Interview

Once you have whittled down a short list of five to ten candidates, the next step should be a telephone interview, which will allow you to gauge their language skills. Canada is still a country of immigrants and because the majority of positions in the dental practice are customer-service related, language skills are important. In a very short phone interview, you'll be able to quickly gauge whether a candidate can understand questions and formulate a relevant response.

Once you have whittled down a short list of five to ten candidates, the next step should be a telephone interview, which will allow you to gauge their language skills.

I usually ask two to three questions in a phone interview. The first concerns what made the candidate apply for the position. The answer allows me to gauge the candidate's passion for the position advertised. In dental offices, the majority of candidates come from within the dental industry, so it is important to know why they are looking for a new job and why they applied to your practice.

The second question concerns what they like most about the work they do. For instance, if you advertised for a dental assistant, the candidates' answer should tell you what they like most about dental assisting, what they are passionate about.

Tip: Remember that candidates may tell you what they think you want to hear, so take each answer with a grain of salt. This is especially true of questions asked over the phone, because you are not able to gauge body language.

There are very few positions in a dental practice that do not require communicating with a patient. Therefore, if candidates are not passionate about patient care or service, it's going to be very difficult for them to integrate into a practice that has a service element as its purpose or part of its purpose.

Tip: It is important that the candidate speak to patient care or service.

The third question I usually ask concerns how the candidates would handle an upset patient. This allows them to demonstrate two skills that are very important for working in a dental practice. The first is thinking on one's feet. In a phone interview, candidates won't expect this type of question, so you can test how quickly they're able to analyze the question and formalize a reply that makes sense. It also allows you, of course, to see whether their approach to customer service fits with your practice's purpose, vision, and customer service ethic. However, if you are hiring a bookkeeper, who will never communicate with clients, the question needs to reflect how the candidates deal with a complex and difficult situation in their area of expertise.

If the candidate has proficient language skills and answers these three questions well, book an in-person interview.

IN-PERSON INTERVIEWS

In-person interviews are the responsibility of dental owners unless they have a knowledgeable and trustworthy office manager. A rule of thumb when interviewing for a dental practice is to schedule interviews outside the practice's working hours. While after-hours interviews eat into the free time of the owner, they don't hurt income and production. They also set the tone that production time is important and should not be disrupted.

I recommend informal interviews to put the candidates at ease.

I usually ask two types of question in interviews. The first relates to understanding what tasks the candidates carried out and what skills they used in their previous position. It's important to know this because each dental practice is a little different, and this information will help to identify what type of training will be needed if the candidate is hired.

The second type of question is behavioral and therefore gives you a glimpse of the candidate's personality, which is important to ensure that the new hire fits your practice's culture, the personalities of the existing team, and the purpose of the practice. Past behaviour is usually a good predictor of future behaviour.

Tip: Hire based on personality and not strictly on skills. If the employee has the right personality, passion, and drive, skills can be taught.

MOTIVATION

Once you've hired your staff members, your next responsibility is to motivate them. How this is done will depend on your personality, as the owner/dentist or as the office manager.

Motivating new hires involves a mixture of factors. It necessitates purpose alignment: the employee's purpose is aligned with that of the clinic. It demands recognizing the stressors we discussed in the last chapter. It demands the provision of perks and an effective financial remuneration structure. For example, in the company I run, I offer a $500/year contribution to any type of continuing education employees choose to undertake. It doesn't have to be in their area of work. I believe that enhancing knowledge can result in transferable skills, which makes this perk mutually beneficial.

It's important to match the right perks to your practice. Common perks include enhanced health and dental benefits, paid vacations, extended paid vacation time, and periodic bonuses. When deciding on which perks to offer, other parameters, such as geographical location, competition for employees (i.e., how many skilled individuals are available in your geographic area) and employee interests should be taken into consideration.

Of course, these motivating factors apply to existing employees as well as new hires.

FIRING

One of the more stressful tasks in a dental practice is firing employees. Not only does this create a tense situation between the owner and the employee but it also creates a vacuum that has to be filled: work must be reassigned to other employees, at least temporarily.

In addition to this stress, there is the matter of labor laws and legislation. Canada is governed by two major pieces of legislation: Provincial Employment Standards and the Human Rights Act. Provincial Employment Standards are enforced provincially and set the minimum standards required under labor law to be provided to employees. The Human Rights Act is federally governed and cases under this act are handled in civil courts. Most businesses pay attention to employment standards, but few take into account the Human Rights Act and its potential implications for their business.

It is very important that you are familiar with the labor standards in your province and with human rights legislation, which has both federal and provincial/territorial jurisdiction.

It is very important that you are familiar with the labor standards in your province and with human rights legislation, which has both federal and provincial/territorial jurisdiction. Federal human rights legislation and other labor-related regulations in Canada are designed to protect the employee. Therefore, dealing with employees means dealing with labor laws and human rights legislation. It is crucial that you have the right tools to address particular employee issues. Make sure you have good legal counsel, such as LegalShield, which offers free legal counseling services over the phone for a low monthly fee. We will look at regulatory issues in a bit more detail in Chapter 8.

Keeping a detailed employee file helps ensure that you are properly equipped to address a claim in the event any employees pursue legal action. This file should include all professional interactions with the employees, staff memos, periodic performance reviews, and your own observation of their overall performance and conscientiousness.

When terminating an employee, you should include an exit interview, in which you both try to understand and agree on the reason(s) for the employee's departure, his or her pay-out, and record of employment (ROE) submission to the government. It's important that the staff also understand why an employee left in order to eliminate any possibility that those who remain feel insecure in their jobs. Chances are that most will realize why the employee was not a good fit. Remember that, as the owner, you are responsible for the ethical and legal behavior of the corporation you head and this includes the behavior of your employees.

Tip: Include another individual (preferably of the opposite sex) in the exit interview/firing meeting. This can prevent a sexual-harassment claim by the (ex)employee or a claim that the meeting was held under duress.

It is not in your interest to end up in court, yet a lot of dentists end up in court after being sued by ex-employees. It doesn't really matter if you win in court. Whether it's because of legal fees, time wasted, or the impact on your reputation, if you end up in court, you've lost.

WHAT MATTERS MOST

Dr. Neville is one of the nicest people I know, but she is also a little naïve. Her story begins when she finished her association with a practice in Vancouver to build a new clinic in Greater Vancouver. She hired an office manager and established expectations, including the office manager's responsibility for handling all HR issues in the practice. Over the course of three years, the office manager fired three employees: two hygienists and one receptionist. The three got together and filed a human rights complaint in the civil courts on the basis that they were not warned before being fired.

Dr. Neville was not aware of the circumstances of the employee's departure and relied on the office manager, who had no experience of firing people and acted on hunches when determining what was right in a situation. Nine months, three court appearances, and $4,400 in legal fees later, Dr. Neville settled with all three employees, and then fired her office manager in accordance with labor laws and regulations.

She had to pay more than $40,000 in fines to the employees and Crown for improper handling of employment termination. The office manager had recorded the code for lay-off on the records of employment, which indicated that the employees had been released due to lack of work, and part of the fine was due to this being a false claim. I recommend that you never take this route, even if it causes less immediate conflict in your practice. You are providing the government with false information and this is illegal. However difficult it may be, you must deal with HR issues with clarity and honesty.

Tip: Make a conscious effort to get to know people who work for the non-dental regulatory bodies. These include those concerned with employment standards, public health, privacy, and staff at the Canada Revenue Agency (CRA). The more of these individuals you know and the stronger your relationship with them is, the more prepared you will be to tackle situations and the less surprised you will be with regulation changes.

Regardless of how busy you are, make sure that the person responsible for HR understands regulations and proper practice. Be aware of everything that is being done on behalf of your practice. Make sure records of employment, in particular, are accurate and updated, and make sure that your HR person runs by you potentially litigious actions prior to taking action. Just because you have hired people and assigned tasks does not make you less responsible in the eyes of the law. Ultimately, it is your responsibility to ensure your practice acts in compliance with the law.

CHAPTER 6

CUSTOMER SERVICE

One of the biggest challenges in dental clinics is having front staff who can welcome patients properly and ensure that the patient experience is a pleasant one.

Why is this so difficult? The main reason is that the front staff are responsible for everything that is not clinical in a dental clinic, from taking payments to calling patients to verify their upcoming appointments and dealing with insurance companies. Despite this workload, they must make time to ensure that patients are being properly accommodated, greeted with a smile, feel welcomed, and given the attention they need.

One clinic in Calgary identified this as a major limitation. Their solution was the creation of the new position of greeter, which is similar to that of a concierge, who welcomes each patron to the clinic. This person's job is to ensure the patient feels comfortable and looked after, has water and coffee available, and knows what to do and where to go in the office. The greeter is also responsible for the cleanliness and appeal of the waiting area.

This position incurs an additional expense, but a loyal patient base is worth far more than the $30,000 to $35,000 a greeter's salary costs each year. Loyal and happy patients bring friends and family and bolster the reputation of your clinic, which means this investment can set you apart from the competition in terms of level of service. Investing in your practice and having the right staff in the right positions pay off in the long run. Take advantage of everything that helps you reach your goals. If this approach is in line with your purpose, I recommend you consider it as a solution to your customer service needs.

Whether you are a dentist, office manager, or receptionist, you will interact with patients to resolve problems and provide care in order to retain loyal patients and attract new ones through patient evangelism (word of mouth). The White House Office of Consumer Affairs found that losing a customer is costly: it is six to seven times more expensive to acquire a new customer than it is to keep a current one,[8] and since news of bad customer service reaches more than twice as many ears as praise for a good service experience,[9] customer service skills and human interaction are paramount to a successful practice.

Despite its significance, there is a misconception about what customer service actually is. We have come to accept that customer service is the act of providing a resolution to a client's problem. This is a mistake; customer service is about conveying to patients

---

8   The White House Office of Consumer Affairs, "75 Customer Service Facts, Quotes & Statistics," n.d., *HelpScout*, available at https://www.helpscout.net/75-customer-service-facts-quotes-statistics/.

9   The White House Office of Consumer Affairs, "75 Customer Service Facts, Quotes & Statistics," n.d., *HelpScout*, available at https://www.helpscout.net/75-customer-service-facts-quotes-statistics/.

the feeling that a trustworthy person is looking out for their best interests. Providing solutions to problems is only part of the story.

I recently conducted an informal phone survey of professionals, from executive directors to Customer Service Association officers and front-of-office staff in service businesses. I asked them what they thought customer service is.

Their replies showed why customer service is the weakest link in most businesses. The majority replied that customer service was about being able to resolve the client's problem in a reasonable time frame. In my experience, real customer service comes into play when you are not able to provide a solution or when all the possible solutions are not what the client wants to hear. In other words, the lower the chance of a resolution, the higher the customer service skill level needed. When there is no amicable solution, ensuring that your client will still trust you demands a very high level of customer service. You must still be seen as a partner in the situation, not just the bearer of bad news. The way you present the outcome, for good or bad, allows clients to separate the bad situation from the service they have received. If a client can come away saying, "The situation we were in was dire, but the customer service rep was able to keep us in the loop and guide us through these terrible times," then you are providing top-notch customer service.

> **The lower the chance of a resolution, the higher the customer service skill level needed. When there is no amicable solution, ensuring that your client will still trust you demands a very high level of customer service.**

In short, in easily resolvable situations, customer service skills are rarely needed. They are required in situations where there is no immediate solution.

ACHIEVING GREAT CUSTOMER SERVICE

There are five components of achieving great customer service. Three are key steps that every customer service representative should take to benefit the client and, ultimately, the practice. Likewise, there are two mindsets that should be adopted in order to achieve superior customer service:

The Three Steps of Great Customer Service:
1. Empathy
2. Getting to the Real Problem
3. Continuous and Consistent Follow-up

1. Empathy

Empathy is the ability to understand and share the feelings of another, which is easier said than done. Many people confuse empathy with sympathy, but to succeed in customer service, it is important to understand the differences between the two. Brené Brown's[10] animated film about empathy and sympathy explains the differences very well. Empathy means relating to people and genuinely wanting to help them. You need to acknowledge patients' issues

You need to acknowledge patients' issues and assure them that they are being heard and are not alone even if you can't help them.

---

10   *Brené Brown on Empathy,* available at https://www.youtube.com/watch?v=1Evwgu369Jw.

and assure them that they are being heard and are not alone even if you can't help them. This is crucial as it establishes a relationship with the patients and opens up a window to properly communicate with them.

2. Getting to the Real Problem

Problems occur when you ask the wrong questions. "What problem are you experiencing?" may be the worst question to ask as the answer only provides you with the patient's interpretation of the problem, which is rarely helpful. Taking the patient's proposed solution and running with it is another unhelpful approach. The patient does not have the training or knowledge to devise the best solution to the issue.

To get to the heart of the problem, you need to get two pieces of information from the patient.

> "What problem are you experiencing?" may be the worst question to ask as the answer only provides you with the patient's interpretation of the problem, which is rarely helpful.

1. You need to know what the patient was trying to achieve. This might be counter-intuitive for some, but having individuals explain in their own language what they are trying to achieve can reveal the proper solution.

2. You also need to know what had been happening before the problem was discovered. This can point to the optimal resolution.

3. Continuous and Consistent Follow-Up

After you've taken steps 1 and 2, it is important that you continue to follow up until you achieve a resolution. If there has been no progress, it's even more important to communicate with the patient to show that he or she is not forgotten and that you are working hard on finding a resolution. This will give the complainant more confidence and trust in you.

Individuals who provide customer service on a daily basis know that providing the highest level of customer service involves hard work and constant effort. It is about providing service, not just solutions.

4. Discretion

Effective communication is key to good customer service, and this does not include gossip. I've heard dentists and assistants talking about a problem with a front-of-office staff member while treating a patient. How uncomfortable would that patient feel when walking back to the front of the dental office and speaking with that person? Another incident involved two staff members talking about the dentist. How would the patient feel in that dentist's chair? It's crucial to the professionalism of your practice and your patients' perception of your professionalism that you do not engage in gossip while a patient is in the chair.

Although privacy, in terms of patient medical records, is generally understood, I've experienced open-space operatories, where patient consultations can be heard in four other operatories. This means other people can hear private, sensitive health information. This is a bad setup.

Similarly, discussing the previous or next patient while treating the current one is very bad practice. Not only is it rude but it may also make the current patient feel less important, and it violates privacy laws. Make sure you only discuss issues that are related to the patient in front of you.

5. Sincerity

Customer service is often called a soft skill or one that is teachable over time. However, time and training will not compensate for a lack of genuine desire to help people. For effective customer service, you need to hire staff members who are willing to put in the daily effort of showing empathy and compassion, listening, and wanting to be part of the solution. It can't be faked for long. For someone who interacts with patients all day long, sincerity will show in body language, attitude, and tone of voice.

Remember technology is available as a great tool to assist your and your team in delivering exceptional service. From the basic patient management software to patient communication tools and phone services that provide you with details about the caller before you even pick up the handset, there are many tools out there to help your team differentiate your practice and earn loyal patients for life. We'll discuss some of these tools further in Chapter 8.

WHAT MATTERS MOST

If you take only one thing from this chapter, it should be the fact that true customer service is all about sincerity. It is obvious when someone is not genuine.

I met Amber at a seminar. She had been jumping from one job to another and was extremely frustrated with not being able to find her place. She had come from the hospitality industry and felt she had exceptional customer service skills. However, when I asked her why she came to the dental industry, she said she wanted to stop dealing with demanding clients and work better hours

Did she have it all wrong? All positions in a clinic provide patient care and service, and if there is a skill that is a must in the dental industry, it is customer service.

I told Amber that if she were tired of providing service, the patients, staff, and owner would sense her actions were not genuine and were inconsistent with what dental practices expect today. This was the reason she was unhappy at work and couldn't keep a job for more than six months.

A year and two jobs later, Amber decided to leave the dental industry and found her place in an assistant bookkeeper position, which had no client interaction. Her story is an example of why sincerity is key to good customer service, but it also illustrates the importance of knowing your *why* (your purpose). Amber did not know her own purpose and that led her down the wrong path. Once she was able to reflect and identify why jobs were not working out for her, she was able to find her purpose, feel fulfilled, and be happy with herself and her work.

Remember to be genuine, and you will not only help other people in need but enjoy a constantly warm and fuzzy feeling.

CHAPTER 7

MARKETING AND BRANDING

By the time Dr. Cantona was in his early forties, he had owned a clinic for over seven years. He had a loyal and intelligent staff of a receptionist and assistant.

He was doing his own hygiene procedures because he was not busy with treatments. He told himself that he enjoyed the variety and did not have enough patients to justify hiring a hygienist.

His dream was to work part-time, while having a fully booked practice staffed by other dentists and hygienists. He wasn't able to pinpoint the problem in order to fix it and so continued with his day-to-day grind.

When I looked at Dr. Cantona's patient base and saw he did not have enough active patients to justify a hygienist, I suggested marketing. He resisted the idea, saying he didn't have the money to spend on marketing. A common myth about marketing is that it costs a fortune, but you don't need a Super Bowl ad to market effectively.

A common myth about marketing is that it costs a fortune, but you don't need a Super Bowl ad to market effectively.

People confuse or associate marketing with either sales or advertising, both of which are components of marketing. However, one of the best definitions of marketing comes from renowned business guru Peter Drucker: "Marketing is not only much broader than selling; it is not a specialized activity at all ... It is the whole business seen from the point of view of its final result, that is from the customer's point of view ... Concern and responsibility for marketing must therefore permeate all areas of the enterprise."[11]

Marketing concerns everything from staff, the office setup, advertising, and, in the case of a dental clinic, how everything looks or is experienced by the patient or potential patient. These elements create an environment where clarity of purpose and consistency are part of the marketing experience.

Marketing for a small, local business can cost you next to nothing. Therefore, after providing Dr. Cantona with a marketing audit, I could convince him to allocate $500 a year to a marketing budget.

Creating websites no longer costs thousands of dollars. Today, you can have a professional website for under $35/month. You can have a professional logo designed for your clinic through an online service such as fiverr.com for $5 to $10. You can open social media

---

11   M. Brenner, "Marketing Is Business: The Wisdom of Peter Drucker," Marketing Insider Group, December 1, 2011, available at https://marketinginsidergroup. com/strategy/marketing-is-business-the-wisdom-of-peter-drucker/.

accounts and set up a Google business page for free. Both of these are good compliments to your own website.

Online content rules today's world, which makes blogging important to your online presence. It is a good idea to spend about a half an hour every two weeks writing a short article or blog. If you don't feel comfortable with this, you can hire a company to populate your website with content, for a fee.

All of this work will pay off in the end, but you won't see new patients right away. It takes time to establish your reach and presence. It took four months for Dr. Cantona to see new patients coming in. They found his practice either through a Google local search or through good reviews on his Facebook page. It took another two and a half years for him to get to a point where he could work part-time.

Here are the main takeaways from this story:

1. Marketing doesn't have to be costly to be effective.

2. There is no cookie-cutter solution; each clinic has its own success formula that depends on its unique environment.

3. As Thomas Edison said, "Vision without execution is just hallucination."[12]

PASSIVE AND ACTIVE INTERACTIONS

Marketing experience comes from passive and active interactions. In passive interactions, a patient, or a potential patient, comes into contact with the practice brand or name through an advertisement. It's an interaction that has nothing to do with the staff. Passive interactions

---

12   B. Stolle, "Vision without Execution Is Just Hallucination," Forbes.com, July 22, 2014, available at https://www.forbes.com/sites/bryanstolle/2014/07/22/vision-without-execution-is-just-hallucination/#37d3b8617446.

include advertisements in magazines, online ads, billboards, signage, flyers, promotions, coupons, and word of mouth. These interactions must reflect the purpose of the practice, which means that creating a consistent experience across interactions is important.

Each interaction, whether active or passive, should elicit the same positive feeling.

Active interactions are those in which the individual interacts with staff or people who represent the clinic. These are in-person interactions.

Each interaction, whether active or passive, should elicit the same positive feeling.

MARKETING AND BRANDING

In the context of a dental clinic, marketing is foremost about branding and positioning.

Your actual brand includes what people think about when they hear your brand name. In other words, branding is the intangible sum of the attributes of your product or service.

Branding

What is a brand? People often say that your brand is the name of your clinic, but this is a mistake. Your actual brand includes what people think about when they hear your brand name. In other words, branding is the intangible sum of the attributes of your product or service.

Your brand usually contains a combination of words and design: the design of the logo, your color scheme, the wording and phrasing of your ads, the design of the office, and the phrasing on the various forms and applications used by the clinic, including how staff answer the phone or interact with patients. All of that creates the brand.

Many elements go into creating a full and a strong brand, but the most important and relevant to the dental businesses are originality, sincerity, and visibility, which is connected to positioning and online presence.

Originality

Originality means having a unique and original message. Having a purpose helps substantially in creating an original message for your practice. Likewise, your brand must communicate the purpose very clearly and consistently through originality.

Sincerity

Secondly, your brand must convey sincerity. Today, people interact with so many different companies and brands that it's important to always be yourself and reply to posts about you on the Internet. For example, on TripAdvisor, hotel managers (or someone from the hotel using the hotel manager's name) will often reply with a canned response whether the review is good or bad. The structure of their reply is the same, but they change two or three words depending on whether it's a good or bad review. This causes readers to lose their connection with the brand because this interaction seems robotic.

Example 1:
Hotel with lots of contrasts

Hotel has beautiful views on the Niagara Falls side. You just want to sleep with curtains open. On the other hand this hotel is OVERpriced, and is in great need of immediate renovations and better furniture.

Thank Zori H

Response from General Manager

Responded 2 days ago

We appreciate you choosing our hotel for your recent stay in the area. We are happy you enjoyed your stay. We hope that if you return to the area, you will give us another try. Thank you.

Example 2:

Disappointed That the Internet Wasn't Working Right

Switched to this hotel at the last minute in order to stay at a property with a view of the Falls. The room was fine, although the beds were a little soft for us. Beautiful view of the Falls as well.

Thanks FlynLass1

Response from General Manager

Responded 2 days ago

Thank you for choosing our hotel for your recent stay. I do apologize for the concerns you had with the Wi-Fi. I do hope that if you return to the area, you will give us another try. Thank you.

These are two reviews on the same website made by the same hotel manager. Do you get a feeling that he cares about the experience of these people and their feedback? Do you feel that he genuinely and eagerly awaits their arrival next time? Or do you get the feeling that this person copies and pastes, which risks destroying the hotel's appeal to future guests.

To be sincere, you should reply to good and bad reviews as if they were given in person. Listen to the feedback, understand it, and improve. With unique responses, the reviewer gets a feeling that someone invested time and effort into listening to them and wants to be better. This is important and solidifies relationships and connection to a brand.

Bad reviews are the nature of any business, and a dental clinic is no exception. The way you respond to a negative review is what sets you apart. Your response needs to be consistent with your purpose and with who you are, and it needs to show you accept feedback and have a genuine willingness to make things better.

Bad reviews are the nature of any business, and a dental clinic is no exception. The way you respond to a negative review is what sets you apart.

Many who read a bad review also read the reply. Even if you're the best dentist, you'll sometimes have a problem with your diagnosis or treatment. How you handle those particular instances will affect a potential patient's decision to use your services. Keep in mind that 100 percent positive reviews can appear to be fake, so don't worry about one that is less than stellar, as this will also allow you the opportunity to respond appropriately.

Regardless of whether you are advertising on a billboard or responding to a review, always be sincere, genuine, and true to yourself and your purpose.

Visibility

The third element of branding is visibility. You can be original, sincere, and consistent but if no one sees you, no one knows about you. You need to create awareness. If people see your brand's ad 100 times a day on various channels, they will think about your brand, hopefully in a positive way.

Your brand needs to be visible to get as many impressions as possible. Repetition is key. If your brand message is consistent throughout passive and active interactions, it will be engraved on people's minds. Seeing your brand ads across multiple channels is important to this end. Therefore, build a website, run retargeting campaigns, have your ads show up on YouTube videos, get listed on review sites, become active in social media and on billboards, support community events that are consistent with your purpose, book speaking engagements, and write a book. In each case, you can expose a potential patient to your message and control the perception of your brand. The ultimate goal is to create an understanding of your brand, why it's needed, and why it's right for patients.

Build a website, run retargeting campaigns, have your ads show up on YouTube videos, get listed on review sites, become active in social media and on billboards, support community events that are consistent with your purpose, book speaking engagements, and write a book.

Positioning

The objective of positioning is to convince people to view your brand more favorably than competing brands. Practices apply this strategy by emphasizing their distinguishing features. However, once a brand is positioned, its credibility may be destroyed if the brand is repositioned.

Positioning reflects the purpose you've already established for your practice and can be achieved through advertising and other marketing activities. It must present a differentiator, which is the element that sets your services apart from others. Every dentist provides dental treatments as well as diagnostic and dental services. So how can a patient distinguish your practice from that of another dentist? How can patients find out if the clinic's purpose and values match theirs? This is where the differentiator comes into play.

Some provinces in Canada put limitations on clinics' advertising, which makes establishing differentiators challenging. Provincial associations broadly advertise dentistry to the general public, but that doesn't take into account the differences between individual clinics and their need to recruit new patients through advertisements unique to each clinic. This makes it even more important to establish a purpose around which your brand revolves.

Essentially, if your brand is modern and clean, this feeling needs to be infused in the patients from the design and the colors you use in your waiting area to the logo and reading material available. Everything should be designed to create a consistent message throughout.

For example, if a dentist is ecology focused, the entire practice needs to reflect this. This means using tools made from recycled materials, biodegradable gloves, and environmentally friendly dental materials, including e-forms, and reminder e-cards. This would also mean becoming involved with environmental initiatives and groups. This has nothing to do with the actual dental service provided but has everything to do with the practice's purpose. Advertising eco-friendliness positions the brand to attract patients who share this purpose. If they want to support a greener world, they'll come to you rather than a competitor.

Your location is also important. If you buy a practice, you are inheriting a location, which means you need to consider the type of population in that area, the type of population in the existing practice, and what effect that will have on your kind of practice.

For example, Kelowna in British Columbia is an aging city. Most students there don't have insurance coverage, and the elderly there mainly need a denturist/hygienist, not a dentist. Therefore, if you're looking to open a practice in Kelowna and want to make it a hipster kind of practice, you will likely find that people are not connecting with your purpose. At some point, younger families may come to Kelowna and change the demographics there, but until that happens, opening a practice that focuses on pediatric patients might not be the best idea.

Remember that marketing, branding, advertising, and positioning are tools you can use to broadcast you message to the world and attract appropriate patients.

Online Presence: Authority Marketing

Another essential element of your online presence is authority marketing and the easiest way to do this is by adding a blog to your website. Having relevant content creates value for readers on many levels. It raises your practice's ranking in online searches. It allows your existing patients to get a better understanding of the oral health issues you write about, and it can establish you as an authority, which can attract new patients.

For example, if patients of competitor dentists are diagnosed with a dental problem, they will likely Google their condition to learn more about it. If you have posted an article on your blog site that discusses different treatments for this condition, the patients may come to you for a second opinion or even come for treatment, especially if their current dentist doesn't offer those options.

I don't recommend forcing staff members to write blogs; it is better that the content be written by you, the dentist. At the end of the day, a dental practice sells dental services and the blog shows that the dentist knows what he or she is talking about. Add a Book an Appointment button and you've created a relevant and easy way to attract new patients to your practice.

> If patients of competitor dentists are diagnosed with a dental problem, they will likely Google their condition to learn more about it. If you have posted an article on your blog site that discusses different treatments for this condition, the patients may come to you for a second opinion or even come for treatment, especially if their current dentist doesn't offer those options.

WHAT MATTERS MOST

It is important to know both what works and what you should avoid when it comes to marketing.

Don't overlook purpose alignment. It ensures that everything in your practice reflects your purpose and is consistent. Any communication that is not in line with your purpose creates confusion for the brand and weakens it.

Tip 1: When evaluating a marketing piece (even clinic design), ask yourself and your team, "Does it reflect our purpose?" If it does, run it; if it doesn't, redo it until it does.

Staff buy-in is key to consistency across channels. However, consistency will never be achieved if your staff does not buy into the purpose and the subsequent marketing campaigns.

Tip 2: Get feedback from your team about your marketing activities and their alignment with the practice's purpose. The team's involvement helps them to feel they are an integral part of the overall marketing strategy and makes it easier for them to buy into the idea of marketing.

Tip 3: Keep your staff in the loop of *all* communication going out. They are your front-line team and should never be kept in the dark about the communication going out to existing and/or potential patients.

Make sure you measure your marketing campaigns to determine whether they were a success or failure. This also allows you to spend money where it counts and have a better return on investment.

Tip 4: Put unique codes or "secret words" on your marketing campaign materials for patients to mention (and your staff to track), so that you can measure the effectiveness of each effort to bring existing or new patients into the clinic.

Tip 5: For digital marketing campaigns, create a separate landing page for each and measure the traffic to see how effective each campaign is.

Community engagement is important to your marketing strategy and customer outreach. A dental clinic is a brick-and-mortar business with a fixed location and therefore attracts patients in the geographical area of the clinic. Community engagement can involve sponsoring community events, supporting a local charity, and having staff volunteer their time.

Tip 6: A particularly helpful marketing tactic involves spending time in schools and teaching children about proper brushing. The kids take a branded calendar home to put on the fridge and are given a challenge to mark down every day they brush their teeth. This results in brand exposure, as your logo and calendar are in front of all family members, and you have directly contributed to better oral health for you community.

We will take a more in-depth look at the variety of tools you can use to increase the success of your practice in the next chapter.

CHAPTER 8

TOOLS YOU SHOULD BE USING

Although a dentist is a medical specialist, with little knowledge of business practices that are needed to support a dental practice, your practice can really shine. Responsible dental owners should be familiar with the many tools at their disposal. As they become more familiar with the tools, they'll be better equipped to take care of their practice and patients.

In addition to dental owners' responsibility for all things medical, they must also provide a safe workplace for employees, patients, and vendors, which includes understanding finance, regulations, requirements for physical safety, and the creation of a bully-free and sexual-harassment-free environment. Since they can't be expected to be experts in all these areas, they need to work with trusted specialists, which will allow them to minimize risk and increase compliance. Specialists' professional advice on potential risks is necessary.

How do you find those specialists? In this chapter, we'll explore the tools that facilitate dealing with third-party vendors, and understanding hard numbers, remuneration structures, and technology.

THIRD-PARTY VENDORS YOU NEED

There are six main categories of vendors that a dental practice needs:

- legal

- accounting

- financial

- dental regulatory

- non-dental regulatory

- value-adding organizations

Legal

It is imperative to have good legal counsel, but it is best to have more than one legal advisor because each will advise you based on his or her specific knowledge and experience. We use a service called LegalShield[13], which is available in Canada and most US states. It offers general advice at a lower cost and is a good way to supplement more specialized corporate legal counsel to better understand your legal responsibilities and liabilities.

---

13   No personal profit is made by recommending any companies or products mentioned in this book.

Accounting

An accountant's job includes advising you on best way to document your income in accordance with tax regulations. A good accountant can save you thousands of dollars on your tax returns, while a mediocre accountant may cost you thousands of dollars or even a CRA audit.

Your accountant should be well versed in CRA regulations in Canada or IRS regulations in the USA. For instance, the Canadian government is currently deliberating some tax changes that may substantially impact small businesses, dental clinics included. Therefore, having a good accountant who can prepare and help you make the right decisions once these changes are finalized is imperative.

It is also advisable to have more than one accountant to turn to for advice. I recommend BDO, which offers an accountant referral service or the option to purchase accounting services on an ad-hoc basis. You can compare their recommendations with those of your existing corporate accountant to ensure you are getting the best advice.

Financial

Financial advice can be found not only through banks but any establishment that deals with money, as well as, of course, portfolio and wealth planners and investor groups, among others. In this section, we will look at three financial categories: invested funds, liquidated or free cash, and debt.

1. Invested Funds

Invested funds are those invested in stocks, bonds, real estate, or other products that yield a return. You can't liquidate them rapidly.

In addition to the many financial establishments available to help you invest your money, properly certified accountants can also help you.

2. Liquidated Cash

Liquidated or free cash is cash that's sitting in your bank account. A dental practice should keep three months' worth of operational costs in the bank as liquid cash and a further 20 percent of this amount in liquid assets. For example, if your operating costs are $10,000 a month, you need to keep $30,000 in the bank and $6000 in liquid assets. It is your lifeline for unexpected expenses. Cash allows you to make mistakes and not suffer extreme consequences, as Dr. Hernandez did.

Dr. Hernandez had a viable dental practice for many years, but when he died suddenly at the age of forty-five, his heirs found he had no cash available. The dentist had heavily invested in real estate and a long-term investment portfolio. The heirs had no cash to cover short-term expenses. By the time they had gained control over his estate, could liquidate assets, and act on behalf of the practice, including issuing paychecks, the majority of employees had left, and many of the patients had gone elsewhere to receive a timely solution for their oral needs. It was too late to recover the practice from this slump, and the heirs had no choice but to close the business and sell some of the equipment to other practices. Dr. Hernandez's story highlights important points about risk management and contingency planning.

Investment advisors, regardless of which type you work with, will offer you the opportunity to invest your liquid cash, but this only makes sense if 1) you are able to get back the cash within a forty-eight-hour turnaround to minimize your risk of not having cash when you need it, and 2) you understand in detail and are comfortable with where your money is being invested.

3. Debt

Many of us follow the old-school model when it comes to debt: we pour all our free income into eliminating our debt as soon as possible. However, debt is not necessarily a bad thing, depending on the financial structure you choose for your practice and your goals. You can work with your accountant to figure out the best financial structure and how to leverage debt to achieve your goals.

With the rock-bottom interest rates we've had for the last fifteen years, having a certain level of corporate debt hasn't been bad. It has allowed us to use other people's money (for example, through banks) to fund our business. Interest can be written off as a tax-deductible expense. To use debt as a cost-effective financial strategy, make sure you have a good financial advisor with a strong track record.

Dental Regulators

Membership of a dental association allows you to develop a good relationship with dental regulators, which in turn offers an opportunity to influence future decisions that affect your business and your ability to deliver top-notch oral health services to the public. Association membership allows you address and resolve any issues you may have and provides advance notice of impending changes in regulations.

Dental associations are also important in allowing you networking opportunities that can be vital to your practice.

Non-Dental Regulators

There are a number of non-dental regulators, including those governing public health, privacy, employment standards, and human rights. In Canada, public health is regulated by provincial governments; privacy is the regulatory domain of federal and provincial governments. Employment standards are set by provincial governments, and human rights are federally governed.

It is important to build relationships with these regulators. They are outside your industry, but they influence your ability to run your practice. For example, Ontario Public Health did inspections and closed eight practices in one geographical area for violations of public health regulations. Human rights regulations govern interactions between your patients and your own staff. A change in regulations could affect your hiring or firing process. Privacy regulations are key to a dental practice. You need to know what information you can and can't disclose, and to whom, and you need to make sure you are compliant with the Personal Information Protection and Electronic Documents Act (PIPEDA), on top of special provincial regulations in Canada, or the Health Insurance Portability and Accountability Act (HIPAA) in the USA.

I highly recommend adhering to these regulations and working with the regulator to solve any conflicts. For example, one regulation requires a particular process for sanitizing hand pieces, but the manufacturer suggests another. In this case, it is important to be able to bring this conflict to the regulator and have it resolved. Otherwise, you risk being penalized if your practice were to be officially inspected.

If you do not know the various non-dental regulations that can affect your practice, you will run into problems. Having relationships with these regulators allows you to ensure that your policies and your processes are compliant with the regulations.

Value-Adding Organizations

A value-adding organization is a company that creates value for the clinic and for the dentist but does not fall under any of the categories we have mentioned so far. It includes companies that provide services related to marketing, information technology (IT), software, payroll, and temporary staff. Janitorial and landlord services are also value-added services. Even the mailman who comes to the practice provides, to an extent, a value-added service.

Identifying these services and establishing a solid relationship with companies that provide them creates more value for your practice and affords access to more vendors you can trust to make your practice successful.

For example, an IT company makes sure you have the proper technology set up and your system works with minimal disruption. IT personnel must understand your processes in order to show you how their software provides solutions to your challenges, and they must make sure you are able to use their software and maximize its utility. Many of your challenges can be solved by intelligent software and exceptional service from the team supplying the software. We will discuss technology later in this chapter.

KNOW YOUR NUMBERS

Knowing your numbers is key to running a successful business. To do this, you need to understand budget, P&L, cash flow, and reporting systems.

I have seen companies go out of business because they misunderstood the differences between P&L and cash flow statements and made the mistake of only looking at one of them. In order to understand the differences between cash flow and profit, you need to understand what a P&L includes and what it does not, and what a cash flow statement shows and what it does not.

At the higher level of tracking your numbers, you will be dealing with budgets and P&L. At the mid-level, your day-to-day operational activity numbers include reports, collections, accounts receivable, and general operations.

You also need to understand numbers related to your personal expenses and the income you have to generate from your business for your personal needs.

This chapter is not designed to make you an accountant, but rather to give you tools to help you understand key numbers and not fear terms such as *budget* and *P&L*. It will also give you an understanding of the importance of P&L and budgets as a management tool. In this way, you can sit with your office manager (or your dentist if you are the office manager) and project business performance in the upcoming year.

Cash Flow

Cash flow relates to the exchange of cash in your bank account: money coming in as it is collected from the patients and insurance companies, and money going out to pay the bills, including those for rent, services rendered, debt principal and interest, equipment leases, consumables, computer maintenance, and hardware.

Common sense says that the best way to stay in business is to make sure your cash flow is positive, which means you have more money coming into the bank account than going out. You should be monitoring this as closely as possible so that you can identify problems as they arise. You should also look at your cash flow when reviewing the P&L.

Profit & Loss

A P&L statement works on a very simple formula: revenue less expenses equals profit. To maximize profit you need to increase revenue and decrease expenses, including rent, utilities, salaries, and interest payments on debt and taxes. What remains after expenses are deducted is your net income.

When you create a budget, you are creating an estimation of how your actual P&L will look for the following year.

P&L does not have a place for your debt payments. However, earnings before interest, depreciation, taxes and amortization (EBIDTA) is the measure that financial organizations use to decide whether to lend you money. You can use this measure to determine whether you are able to generate enough income to pay your debt. For example, one business went bankrupt because it was generating a net income of $160,000 but was paying over $200,000 in principal. This number was not reflected in the P&L, which showed the business as profitable even though it was losing $40,000. The business owners could not figure it out and their accountant did not take time to explain.

There is a synergy between performance (in terms of P&L) and the cash flow statement. Because the majority of dental clinics have some sort of debt, there is a discrepancy between the P&L and the cash flow statement because the P&L does not show payments on the principal of a loan.

Therefore, it is very important when you are reviewing the performance of the company to cross-reference your P&L with the statement of cash flow to make sure it is positive.

Budget

Your budget is a projection; it is never exact, but it is important if you are to manage your business effectively and understand changes in conditions.

I have had many conversations with dentists who said they do not create a budget; their accountant simply figured out their revenue at the end of the year, based on annual performance. I have met office managers who did not know what it meant to create a budget.

Creating a budget is not as frightening as it might seem. It is an estimation of how the upcoming year will look in terms of revenue and expenses. It allows business leaders to take all of their knowledge of the business, historical P&Ls, and plans for the upcoming year, and put them on paper to see what the result (net income) will likely be. Among other things, it can help identify areas of potential expense or revenue.

For example, if you are looking at construction and increasing your physical space to add two operatories, then you know you are going to have a construction expense that will make this year's expenses higher than last year's. Analyzing the numbers will allow you to plan for that.

As another example, if there is a sudden change in population in your area because a new neighborhood is being built and will be occupied by young families, then you know you are going to have more young families as your patients. These are factors you need to incorporate into your business projections.

Budgeting is a very useful tool to project performance. It allows you to compare actual results to budget projections at multiple intervals throughout the year.

To create a budget, start by looking at historical performance. Look at the previous two years and at what the business produced.

What were the expenses and revenue? Now consider everything that you will be doing in the upcoming year. As you go through the year, review your income and expenses and project those numbers in your budget. If discrepancies appear in your projections throughout the year, you will know how to explain them because you will know what influenced them, and you will be prepared to address them.

Operational numbers detail the source of revenue—for example, product sales. They also break down expenses—for example, rental expenses, utilities, consumables, and salaries. As you review those numbers, you are actually looking in detail at the performance of your business.

Let's look at a hypothetical case: Dr. Ibrahimovic is the principal dentist working with an associate and two hygienists. They work five days a week, 9 a.m. to 5 p.m. Both dentists are regularly generating $2 million a year, and both hygienists are contributing a combined total of around $800,000. The hygienists are fully booked and another hygienist is coming on board to ensure all patients are booked for dental hygiene procedures in a timely manner.

In order to accommodate the new hygienist, they have to construct another operatory or extend their office hours, working in shifts and offering evening appointments. Therefore, when creating a budget for the following year, Dr. Ibrahimovic needs to take the new hygienist's production into account, along with the expense of the additional salary and the costs of constructing the new operatory.

Dr. Ibrahimovic is risk averse and this is reflected in his budgeting. He estimates the new hygienist will produce at half capacity for the first six months and at full capacity for the second half of the year.

Let's assume that the new hygienist sees four patients a day for the first six months and eight patients a day for the remainder of the year. We can estimate (conservatively) the increase in production as follows:

(4 patients x 5 days a week x 25 weeks x $200/cleaning)
+ (8 patients x 5 days a week x 25 weeks x $200/cleaning)

$300,000

This example uses fairly rough numbers and a conservative way of budgeting. Feel free to replace the numbers with what makes sense for your practice.

As Dr. Ibrahimovic explains to his new hygienist, "You are expected to generate $100,000 in the first six months of the year. This is when you start seeing patients and begin developing relationships with them. During the following six months, you are expected to produce $200,000. Our admin staff members are here to help book you as fully as possible. Having said that, our goal is 30 percent higher than $300,000—that is, $390,000. So you should ensure that your production is at least three times your salary and you book your patients for their next appointment while they are still in the chair."

You can see from this example that when you are budgeting, you are looking at the expected net profit from hiring a new hygienist. When you hire new staff members, you have to take into consideration whether they will be fully booked right away, what their hours will be, and how they will be paid. And you put all of those calculations into the budget to improve the accuracy of your projection.

Dr. Ibrahimovic's expectation is that each existing hygienist will generate almost $400,000 year. To achieve this goal, they must book their patients' next appointment while they are in the chair, which ensures their production remains at three times their salary.

Individual Numbers

Individual numbers refer to what an individual wants or needs to earn as a reflection of work, effort, and risk. Individual numbers are personal and need to be determined by individuals and their spouse. They have to decide on the lifestyle they want and the income they need to achieve it.

While the federal government has provided a benchmark for what dentists earn, this is a highly subjective area because a dentist's level of income depends on the practice's local population, the dentist's personal goals and values, and a multitude of other variables.

I know a dental owner who is comfortable earning $80,000 a year while spending part of his working hours and a lot of free time assisting remote rural communities with their oral health needs. I know of another dental owner who is comfortable earning $250,000 a year and wants to work as much as possible with patients in complex situations where the impact on their lives is large. I know of another dental owner who is happy earning $100,000 a year, working one day a month in his clinic and spending the rest of his time travelling the world with his family.

Once found, your ideal income must be in line with the other numbers and must make sense for you in terms of the clinic's capabilities and your earning comfort zone. If a dentist knows that his or her lifestyle requires making $200,000 gross, and those numbers do not work with the practice, his or her quality of life will be impacted.

Determining this number starts with what you are comfortable with and then creating a budget for your business, based on realistic expectations.

While this section offers a basic review of the key numbers you need to track to be successful in your business, it's not intended to solve all of your problems. However, it can enhance your awareness and to give you enough knowledge to talk to your advisor and ask pertinent questions. These numbers can be complex and their management can be complex, so it is always a good idea to work with a third-party vendor who specializes in this area. Your advisor will bring his or her expertise to bear, but you need to decide what makes sense and you need to feel in control of what is happening with your business. Just because you are not an accountant does not mean that you should rely on an accountant to read your books and financial reports and interpret them for you. You need to know how to do this yourself so that, at any given point, you know the health of your business.

REMUNERATION STRUCTURES

There is a new trend in dentistry: big corporations are buying up practices and setting goals for production and performance. One unfortunate side effect of this is that dentists are over-treating patients to meet the numbers, while hygienists are under-treating patients to meet their numbers because they have a set one-hour-per-patient system. So instead of making the session a little bit longer because the patient needs more work, they have to move on to the next patient. Besides being unethical, this practice is giving dentistry a bad name.

A dental clinic is a privately owned corporation. It is a business, and it needs to be treated like one. However, it also provides health services, so business numbers should not conflict with providing the proper health care.

Remuneration structures are supposed to motivate employees to be more efficient to meet goals and metrics. You should not compromise patient health to meet them, but you also need to control your business to make sure that it is profitable. Balance is important.

There are different ways to structure the remuneration benefits for hygienists and dentists in your practice: straight salary, base salary with commissions or bonuses, and group bonuses. Each has advantages and disadvantages.

Hygienists

When you pay your employees, particularly hygienists, a straight salary, you are not offering them bonuses or commissions. You pay a slightly higher than average salary and monitor their performance throughout the year. The advantage of this structure is that employees know exactly what they are going to be earning. It is clear and fair for the employee and predictable for the owner. The disadvantage is that it limits the aspirations and ambitions of employees. If they work harder, they are not compensated for it. This can lead to laziness because they are going to be paid regardless of how much or how well they work. This makes measuring performance even more important.

You can offer a base salary plus a commission or a bonus. The salary itself would be lower than a salary alone, but the employees would earn commission based on their individual productivity. The advantage of this system is that individuals have some control over their income. We touched upon internalists and externalists in Chapter 4. This system works well for internalists because they feel that they are able to influence their destiny. Another advantage is that the commission is based on production: if productivity does not increase in order to increase revenue, then the commission is not paid and thus does not increase expenses. A disadvantage is that people can perceive this to be unfair. They see one person get a bigger cheque but may not see the extra work that person did. Again, this makes transparent metrics important. Everyone should be able to see the performance metrics to appreciate that everybody's getting paid according to the work they generated. A disadvantage of this system is the increased cost of staying on top of the metrics and calculating the bonuses. This can be mitigated by having the right software system in place to handle the payroll. We will discuss this later in this chapter. Another disadvantage of this system is that it can lead to the under-treatment of patients by hygienists as they rush through appointments to hit a number. This possibility needs to be monitored by the dentist.

Some dentists give a group bonus. For example, if all staff members meet their metrics, everyone gets $4,000. This is not a solution, because one staff member could complain about working twice as hard as anyone else, and yet they all get the same bonus.

Dentists

The first type of payment to dentists is a straight salary, as it is for hygienists. This is usually applied to young associates who are straight out of school. It provides financial stability while they learn hands-on dentistry without having to worry about production. It reduces the stress of navigating a new work environment and allows them to begin to repay their student debt.

An advantage of this type of payment is that it generally encourages a slightly higher quality of dentistry because the focus is purely on dentistry. It is also a predictable expense for the owner who knows exactly how much has to be paid in salaries. The disadvantage is the cash flow risk that arises. The dentist will have done the work and gotten paid even before the costs are reimbursed by the insurance company, so you could have a cash crisis if the insurance company takes three or four weeks to pay. This is an important consideration, especially if you have a high-volume practice. You need a sizable amount of free cash to bridge the gap while you wait for money to come in. Another disadvantage is that because the dentist is on a straight salary, he might prefer to do only certain treatments—for example, crowns.

When dentists are paid a commission, there is a risk they may choose treatments that yield the most money rather than those that would make more sense for their patients. I have heard stories about dentists telling patients they need eight fillings when they do not. As a dental owner, it is imperative, and your responsibility, to enforce proper ethics within the practice.

Web Tools

Today, it is important to have an online presence. Gone are the days when people picked up the Yellow Pages to find a dentist. In our office, Yellow Pages is used to make the computer monitor higher.

However, there are many ways to create an online footprint for businesses and many of these solutions are free or low cost. Today, people are on social media. They use Google to find businesses in their area. They look at reviews. A lot of dentists do not have an online presence, or they have an outdated website that they paid some company to create years earlier. If this is you, it is time to spruce up your web presence.

Google can give you a free business listing. Just find your business, claim it, and request a postcard with a code be sent to you to verify it is yours. Once you claim it, you can add some pictures and full contact information. When people are looking for a dentist in your area, your listing will appear. It's free and easy to set up, so you should always do this.

There is also a digital Yellow Pages that offers a free business listing. Because it has a good reputation, these listings come up on the first page in search engine results. This makes having a listing here important for your practice. If you use their support to set up this page, the sales rep will try to sell you a lot of services. Just stick to the free listing and make sure the details you post there are consistent with the Google business listing.

Provincial dental associations usually have a Find a Dentist listing for the general public. Make sure that your practice also appears there with information that is consistent across platforms.

It is also important to have social media accounts to interact with the public. You should have at a minimum a Facebook, LinkedIn, Instagram, and Twitter account. These are free and allow you interact with existing patients or new patients.

For a domain service provider, the service that hosts your website, I recommend GoDaddy.com. There are many online guides to help you find a good domain name for your business. A generic domain name, such as Happy Smiles Clinic, might not be available. Find a domain name that is unique to you. I recommend that you do not use words that are easily misspelled, and do not intentionally misspell words. It is also best to avoid hyphens.

There are ways to get a stunning website for under $20 through website builders such as Wix or Wordpress, which have themes that are easy to use. Anyone can create a stunning website cheaply using these services compared to thousands of dollars for a personalized design from a web design company.

Web builder services allow you create a consistent design across all pages. Just make sure your contact information is consistent with your free listings and that the look is consistent with your logo and branding. If you need help here, Fiverr.com offers a service that allows you book a freelancer starting from $5. These designers can create a whole branding suite for $100. Make sure you use your logo everywhere your listing appears and maintain consistency in branding throughout the practice. You should also use your logo on promotional material, business cards, and calendars, and have it embroidered on your scrubs. I use 4Imprint.ca and Vistaprint.ca for our printing needs.

Once you've created your web presence, test its performance by having people Google "dentists" in your area. Unless they live on the other side of the city, your practice should come up in their location search. This will help you ascertain if you campaign is working or needs tweaking.

These are low-cost but effective solutions to achieve consistency in your branding and visibility for your clinic.

Leveraging Technology

Technology continues to evolve and encompass all aspects of our lives and work. In clinical areas, we are looking at 3D printing as a small to medium-size revolution. Within ten years, dental clinics will be able to print bitewings and other plastic sundries as well as complete dentures to specifications.

The future looks exciting. Technology is rapidly evolving, so it is crucial to create a well-rounded experience and squeeze the most out of the technology you have or the technology available to you.

From an HR perspective, technology helps you hire the right people. LinkedIn, the professional social network is a great tool to research candidates, their interests, articles they've written—if any—and groups they are members of, and it allows you to compare their resume to the experience they list. You can also see which of their skills their connections have endorsed, which can give you some insight into their strengths.

Today, job seekers no longer turn to the wanted section in the newspaper to find work. They look at online job boards, follow companies on social media, and read online reviews of these companies by past employees. This type of job seeking offers a great opportunity to find the right employee for your business by reaching them through social media or online job boards.

Management Software

I highly recommend using good management software. Technology also offers online forms and applications for quicker hiring, but you can also benefit from tracking employee files and time clocks (and therefore an easy and consistent payroll system). A tech tool such as MaxiManager allows staff to easily trade shifts. This frees up the office manager's time, allowing him or her to manage the practice and not drown in micro-managing it. I recommend this tool for any clinic that has over five employees. Once you start using it, you will be surprised that you ever managed without it. You can find more information at www.maxidentsoftware.com/maximanager.

Practice management software is a powerful tool that can help you track and manage the three drivers in your clinics. There have been very few major changes to the practice management software industry in the last fifteen years. It is now standard practice to have a digital scheduling system, patient management (billing and personal information), digital charts, and integrated digital X-rays. Even patient communication has become digital. Having a digital system enhances the patient experience, allows your practice to keep accurate records, and saves time by having automated systems at its disposal. I am currently providing a free, fully featured license for Canadian dentists at www.maxidentsoftware.com/freemaxidentlicense.

For quite a while, software companies, mine included, have focused on including value-added services in their main offering—for example, a patient communication service or portal. We have added a mobile app to our patient communication service so that patients can book hygiene appointments and exams on their smartphone.

Image Manipulation

Digital X-rays and 3D sensors have taken the Canadian dental industry by storm. These allow image manipulation, whether zooming in on specific areas, inverting colors, adding contrast, or brightening up the image. X-ray exposure is far lower than that of conventional film machines, so you can take more shots from different angles to insure more accurate diagnosis. Not only are you more efficient but you also show patients that you are on top of new developments, which likely also indicates you are aware of medical advances.

The intra-oral camera is a great addition to your medical records, and it increases the probability of insurance companies approving the treatment. However, its most appealing benefit is that it shows patients their condition. This means they can grasp the severity of the condition, affording you a high buy-in on the treatment. Showing them before-and-after pictures, side by side, also enhances the amount of trust a patient has in you because it indicates that you are focused on their health and well-being and are not over-treating them for their money.

Communication

You can enhance your practice by having an intelligent phone system that identifies callers, their balance, birthday, and next appointment. This is a powerful tool for your front staff. It saves them the time they have to spend looking up the patient's profile. It raises efficiency by providing crucial information in one place so nothing is forgotten and it increases the front staff's confidence level when speaking with the patients over the phone. If you are interested in an intelligent phone system, I recommend visiting **www.maxidentsoftware.com/phoneintegration**.

Call recording is also an important part of your communication system. It offers a way to ensure that exceptional service is delivered to your existing patients and potential patients because patients and staff know their call is being recorded for quality purposes. Psychologically, this ensures staff members monitor what they say on the phone. For this to be effective, you must listen to the calls. It takes time, but it is time well spent because it shows you where staff members might need training. You must secure these recordings with the same level of security you secure for all your electronic health information.

Security

Closed-circuit television (CCTV) is increasingly used in offices and operatories. This allows you to document treatment while a patient is sedated and it also allows you to see what your employees are doing. There have been cases where sedated patients claimed they were sexually abused, which makes CCTV an "insurance policy." Additionally, when people know they are being recorded, they will try to be on their best behavior. Because CCTV has no audio, you do not have to treat it as sensitive patient information. However, you should inform all staff and patients (by means of signage) that they are being monitored on CCTV.

Backing up your data is an important security practice. The more digital records you produce, the greater the risk of something going wrong. I cannot stress enough to dentists and office managers how important it is to have two separate backups and to invest time to ensure the backup is restorable. Two main issues arise when you choose to not validate and verify your backup until a crisis occurs, as the following two scenarios show:

1. You did a recent backup. However, when restoring it, you find out that some of your data wasn't backed up. This happened to multiple clients of mine when they were hit by ransomware. All of their images were encrypted. It was a disaster. After some work, our team was able to restore the images for some, but not all, clients.

2. You did a recent backup. However, when trying to restore it, you find that it fails to restore. This is by far the most frustrating situation.

Unfortunately, little can be done in these scenarios, which is why a proper backup is a lifesaver when everything goes wrong.

There are many other valuable technologies that will enhance your practice, too many to list here. Regardless of how you feel about technology, it is your first and best tool for achieving success in your practice. You should explore what is available and find trusted advisors who can guide you through the jungle of evolving technology.

The tool is only as good as the person who uses it so you should take full advantage of proper training and make sure you work with good vendors. The most important parameter to evaluate when selecting, or researching, the right technology vendor is the employees and their values. When technology breaks down, and it does, the people behind the product make the difference between a minor setback and a complete disaster. To find a good fit in technology partners, there should be synergy between their purpose and yours. You should feel, when interacting with their staff, that they are really looking after you. I have built my company by forming long-term relationships with our clients. I am not interested in a sale if it does not result in a lifelong relationship and an ability to be a key participant in a client's success. When dealing with vendors, you should experience this commitment. This will help you build a team of vendors to help you succeed.

WHAT MATTERS MOST

This chapter aims to provide the dentist with a consolidated description of the basic tools we've talked about throughout this book so that you can implement them in your practice. Each tool provides one small means of achieving your goals that you can implement today. However, with all these tools and recommendations, always ask yourself this question: Does this fit with my purpose? If it does, great. If it does not, change what you are doing until your approach is right for you. As always, if you are dealing in areas beyond your expertise, reach out to reputable third-party vendors who can support your practice with their expertise.

CONCLUSION

Owning and running a dental clinic is stressful and can be overwhelming. When done responsibly, it adds pride, vigor, and a sense of accomplishment.

The first step to responsible dental ownership is finding and defining your purpose. Building a clinic around your purpose ensures less stress, more clarity and a useful tool to use when decisions are required.

"Does this marketing message work?"

"Is this employee performing well?"

"Is this a good reply to a patient's concern?"

All of these questions can be easily answered when you run them by your purpose.

In this book, I have shared relevant business fundamentals together with simple yet powerful tools to help guide your clinic on the path to success. I have explained how patient care of the highest standards can and should co-exist with the right way to conduct business. This is the responsible way to own a dental clinic!

I emphasized the importance of having an office manager who knows what needs to be done and believes in the clinic's purpose.

As of this writing, I can count on one hand the clinics that have a clear purpose and use it consistently with everything they do. Practices that are successful at adhering to their purpose find that balancing exceptional oral care and running a dental business is a breeze. For everyone else, this book is a small part of my effort to help dentists, office managers, and clinics change and achieve success while also living by their purpose and principles.

The right and only way to responsible dental ownership goes through exceptional patient care on both the clinical side and the business side. This only happens when both are given equal importance.

If you are to take only one thing from this book, I would like it to be the ability to think about your clinic in a different way. You and your clinic are responsible for patients' well-being and for employees' families. Having a synergy between your purpose and the clinic's purpose is the way to ensure both patients and employees understand who you are, what you represent, and what you want to achieve. This attracts the right employees and the right patients and will help you become a responsible dental owner who balances business and ethics through purpose.

ABOUT THE AUTHOR

In working with hundreds of dental teams as the CEO of Maxim Software Systems (Maxident Software), Alex believes that a professional and knowledgeable dental office manager is instrumental in having a successful and stress-free dental practice. The need for an education-based organization to connect standardization, certification, knowledge sharing, and a strong community for this profession, has never been clearer.

Forged by business acumen, administrative professionalism, passion for the industry, and the assistance of an experienced team, Alex founded the Dental Office Managers Association to serve as the official body which represents dental office managers Canada-wide.

Alex brings over ten years of management experience in many industries, on top of his MBA from Edinburgh Business School, Heriot-Watt University and a BSc degree from Holon Institute of Technology. He also volunteers as an Advisory Board Member for the Association of MBAs in Canada, and as an Advisory Committee

Member for the Administrative Assistant Program with Red River College in Winnipeg, MB.

Driven by curiosity (and often stubbornness), he always tries to understand everything he comes across. As a leader, Alex believes businesses, in whatever context, have the opportunity to move forward through effective and impactful collaboration. He is passionate about education and pursues any opportunity that comes his way to help people reach their potential through purpose.

Alex moved to Winnipeg, MB in 2012 with his wife.

Printed in the USA
CPSIA information can be obtained
at www.ICGtesting.com
JSHW012035140824
68134JS00033B/3065